INDIAN SNAKE POISONS,

THEIR

NATURE AND EFFECTS

INDIAN SNAKE POISONS,

THEIR

NATURE AND EFFECTS

DY

A. J. WALL M.D. (LOND.)

GYAN

Published by

Gyan Publishing House
5, Ansari Road
Daryaganj, New Delhi-110002
Phone: 011-47034999, 9811692060
E-mail: books@gyanbooks.com

Distribution Network
gyanbooks.com
India, USA, Canada, UK, Australia, France

ISBN : 978-81-212-9822-3 (PB)
First Published, 1883

2nd Impression 2023

Printed at: Gyan Press, Delhi.

INDIAN SNAKE POISONS, THEIR NATURE AND EFFECTS
Author: A. J. WALL

INDIAN SNAKE POISONS,

THEIR

NATURE AND EFFECTS.

BY

A. J. WALL, M.D. (LOND.).

FELLOW OF THE ROYAL COLLEGE OF SURGEONS OF ENGLAND;
OF THE MEDICAL STAFF, H.M.'S INDIAN ARMY.

1883.

TO

SIR JOSEPH FAYRER, K.C.S.I.,

LL.D., M.D., F.R.S., ETC.,

WHO,

WHILST PERFORMING ARDUOUS PUBLIC SERVICES,

HAS LABOURED SO SUCCESSFULLY IN THE

VAST TERRITORY OF TROPICAL PATHOLOGY AS TO UNITE HIS

NAME INSEPARABLY WITH MANY PROVINCES OF IT,

AND ESPECIALLY WITH THAT RELATING TO

THE INDIAN THANATOPHIDIA,

THIS WORK,

INTENDED FOR THE BENEFIT OF OUR ORIENTAL

FELLOW SUBJECTS,

IS DEDICATED,

AS A SLIGHT EXPRESSION OF GRATITUDE

FOR MUCH KINDNESS,

BY

THE AUTHOR.

PREFACE.

The following is an attempt to present in a concise form the chief features of snake-poisoning as seen in India. The object that has been kept in view has been to define, as closely as possible, the conditions on which the mortality from snake-bite depends, both as regards the physiological nature of the poisoning process, and the relations between the reptiles and their victims, so as to indicate the way in which we should best proceed with the hope of diminishing the fearful mortality that exists.

The observations were made by the author in India under the auspices of the Government. It was during the experiments made for the purpose of finding out the exact cause of the fatal results—one of the first steps that must be taken whenever a method of treatment is sought—that the great and numerous differences in the effects of the various poisons became manifest.

Although every effort has been made to test the

various remedies that have been proposed for snake-bite—and they have been very many—it has not been thought necessary to give the unsatisfactory results of the various trials. The effect of potassium permanganate in destroying the activity of cobra-poison when mixed with it before injection was ascertained by the author some four years ago, but frequent experiment has convinced him that as a practical method of treating the constitutional effects of the poison it is of no avail. The recommendations for treatment given have been tested practically, and the circumstances under which the misfortune happens have been constantly borne in mind. Cases of poisoning by snakes do not usually occur in crowded cities with hospitals always open, with every appliance to receive the sufferer, but in the fields where the peasant steps on the lurking reptile, or more frequently still in the remote village where the wife is bitten in a dark corner of her hut by the snake which superstition has compelled her household to protect. Directions for treatment, to be of use, must be adapted to these contingencies.

The snakes mentioned have been referred to, as a rule, by their scientific names. Had vernacular terms been employed it would not have been possible to select any that would have been intelligible except in very limited areas. Thus the *Bungarus cœruleus* is the *Krait* of Bengal, but the *Gedi Paragúdú* of the Coromandel coast. The *Echis carinata* is the *Afaë* of Delhi, the *Kupper* of Scinde, and the *Foorsa* of Bombay. The word *cobra* has been used as it is of general acceptance, though quite unknown in any native dialect; we are indebted for it to our Portuguese predecessors. It is to be regretted that its scientific equivalent is *Naja* instead of *Naga*, as representing more accurately the Sanscrit *Nág*, a serpent, in which it had its origin.

Although the gravity of a case of snake-poisoning can hardly be over-estimated, yet it must be considered full of promise that recovery may follow even the severe hæmorrhages of viperine poisoning. No wound inflicted by a venomous snake can be despised, yet even when symptoms have developed no case should be considered necessarily fatal. It is hoped that the suggestions made may be of practical use to those who have to deal with this awful scourge, and that the facts here demonstrated may form a starting point for some more successful departure.

CONTENTS.

b

LIST OF ILLUSTRATIONS.

INDIAN SNAKE POISONS,

THEIR NATURE AND EFFECTS.

CHAPTER I.

THE PHYSIOLOGICAL EFFECTS OF THE POISON OF THE COBRA (NAJA TRIPUDIANS).

THE inquiry that naturally presents itself first in considering the subject of snake-poisoning is:—How does snake-poison kill? and what are the changes it effects in the animal system? And as a consequence of this:—Is there only one poison common to all snakes, or are there several? Upon the answers to these questions depend both the certain recognition of snake-poisoning when it comes under observation, and the indications that must serve as guides to us in the treatment of it.

To answer these questions, it will be necessary to examine, with great care, the symptoms produced by various poisonous snakes, in order to detect any differences in their effects, paying special attention to those conditions on which the fatal results are dependent, and any prominent signs that will enable us, with certainty, to say if, in a given case, we have really to deal with the results of snake-bite, or not.

As the cobra (*Naja Tripudians*) is at the same time the commonest and the most deadly of all Indian poisonous snakes, it will be best first to consider the symptoms produced by it, and the ways in which its poison may be fatal. To do this it will be necessary to detail a sufficient number of experiments to bring into prominence all the characteristic symptoms of cobra poisoning, and from them to deduce the direct causes of death. We shall then have a standard by which we shall be able to contrast the effects of the poisons of the other species of venomous snakes.

To begin with the symptoms as they occur in human beings; the following is an account, by Dr. Hilson, of a case that came under his own observation:—

"On a night in June, at about half-past 12 o'clock, Dabee, a Hindu punkah coolie, was bitten on the shoulder by a cobra, whilst sleeping. On inspecting the wound, there were found over the prominence of the right deltoid muscle, and about three quarters of an inch apart, two large drops of a clear serous-like fluid tinged with blood, which had apparently oozed from two small punctures, so minute that they could not be perceived by the naked eye. A burning pain was complained of in the neighbourhood of the bite, which rapidly increased in intensity, and extended so as to affect a circular portion of the integument of the size of an ordinary saucer; and, judging from the description given of it, it was very similar in character to that produced by the sting of a scorpion.

"At 12.45 A.M., or about a quarter of an hour after being bitten, he complained of a pain in his shoulder shooting towards his throat and chest, and said he was beginning to feel intoxicated; but there was nothing in his appearance at this time to indicate that he was in any way under the influence of the poison. On the contrary, he was quite calm and collected, and answered all questions intelligently, at the same time that he was fully alive to the danger of his condition. The pupils were not dilated, and they contracted when exposed to the light of a candle; his pulse was normal, and there was no embarrassment of the respiration. About five minutes after, he began to lose control over the muscles of his legs, and staggered when left unsupported. At about 1 o'clock, the paralysis of the legs having increased, the lower jaw began to fall, and frothy and viscid saliva to ooze from the mouth. He also spoke indistinctly, like a man under the influence of liquor. At 1.10 A.M. he began to moan, and shake his head frequently from side to side. The pulse was now somewhat accelerated, but was beating regularly. The respirations were also increased in frequency. He was unable to answer questions, but appeared to be quite conscious. His arms did not seem to be paralysed. At 1.15 A.M., twenty-five minims of liquor ammoniæ were rapidly injected under the skin of the fore-arm; but as this produced no results, the basilic vein was laid bare, and twenty-five minims injected into it.

"The operation caused no amelioration in the symptoms, and the condition was evidently becoming critical. He continued to moan and shake his head from side to side, as if trying to get rid of viscid mucus in his throat. The respirations were laboured, but not stertorous. The external jugular vein of the left side was next exposed, and twenty-five minims of the liquor ammoniæ injected into it; but without producing any good effect. The breathing gradually became slower, and finally ceased at 1.44 A.M., while the heart continued to beat for about one minute longer. No convulsions preceded death, which took place in one hour and five minutes after the infliction of the bite."

From the description given of the snake, there can be no doubt that it was a cobra, and it is clear that the remedy administered had no more effect on the symptoms than it had on the result. It is a good description by a careful observer, and may be taken as a typical example of cobra-poisoning in the human subject.

On the lower animals, from which alone we can learn the details of the poisoning process, and the exact causes on which the fatal results depend, the effects of cobra-poisoning are well seen in the following cases.

Experiment I.

A medium-sized pariah dog had 0·6 cubic centimètre (about 10 minims) of fresh cobra-poison injected subcutaneously.

5.21 P.M. Injection.

5.23 P.M. Lame in the leg in which the injection was made.

5.29 P.M. Lies down, but does not seem affected.

5.35 P.M. Somewhat sleepy.

5.45 P.M. Got up of its own accord; salivation; retching.

5.47 P.M. Staggers about, and hangs down its head.

5.48 P.M. Cannot stand.

5.49 P.M. Sleepy; respirations 40 per minute.

5.52 P.M. Pulse 72.

5.55 P.M. Convulsions.

5.56 to 5.59 P.M. Convulsions.

6.5 P.M. Respirations quite ceased; heart beats 84 per minute; pupils commencing to dilate.

6.7½ P.M. Heart stopped. Dead.

Experiment II.

At 10.46 A.M. a pariah dog was bitten in the thigh by a cobra.

11.14 A.M. Very lame in the bitten limb.

11.27 A.M. Affected by the poison; staggers when it attempts to walk; chewing movement of jaw and lips.

11.28 A.M. Salivation.

11.30 A.M. Pupils somewhat small.

11.31 A.M. Attempting to vomit.

11.35 A.M. Respiration becoming slower.

11.37 A.M. Respirations 16 per minute.

11.38 A.M. Copious salivation.

11.39 A.M. Respirations fallen to 12.

11.40 A.M. Respirations of a jerky character.

11.42 A.M. Tongue hanging out of the mouth.

11.43 to 11.45 A.M. Convulsions.

11.46 A.M. Convulsions lessening.

11.47 A.M. Convulsions stopped.

11.47½ A.M. Respiration completely stopped; pupils dilating.

11.49 A.M. Heart stopped. Dead.

Experiment III.

A pariah dog was watched for about an hour, during which his respirations varied from 40 to 62 a minute. His pulse was 120.

At 11.56 A.M. a very small quantity of fresh cobra virus was injected subcutaneously into the left thigh; the amount injected was about 0·1 cubic centimètre. The dog lay down after the injection, and seemed to take no notice of what had been done.

12.14 P.M. Pulse 108.

12.15 P.M. Respirations 48.

12.26 P.M. Respirations 44, occasionally a deep respiration; dozing.

12.29 P.M. Respirations 36.

12.32 P.M. Respirations 28; very regular; asleep.

12.35 P.M. Respirations 24; respiratory movement very slight; still sleeping.

12.37 P.M. Respirations 24.

12.40 P.M. Respirations 22.

12.43 P.M. Awoke suddenly with a start, probably aroused by flies; chewing movement of lips and jaws.

12.45 P.M. Attempting unsuccessfully to rise; staggered about on his fore-legs.

12.47 P.M. Respirations 26; hardly perceptible, of a somewhat spasmodic character, and lasting an exceedingly short time; salivation.

12.49 P.M. Pupils about normal.

12.50 P.M. Convulsive twitchings of the whole body.

12.52 P.M. Tongue hanging out; convulsions much stronger.

12.55 P.M. No trace of normal respiratory movement, only convulsions: micturition.

12.56 P.M. Pupils slightly contracted.

12.58 P.M. Convulsions are becoming feebler.

12.59 P.M. No convulsive or respiratory movement whatever; pulse 120.

1.1 P.M. Pulse 96; pupils dilating. The only sign of life remaining is the beating of the heart.

1.2 P.M. Pupils fully dilated; heart stopped. Dead.

Experiment IV.

A pariah dog was bitten by a vigorous cobra. The skin in the middle of the dog's back, as near as possible at an equal distance from his fore and hind legs, was taken up, and the cobra injected its poison into it.

8.25 A.M. Infliction of the bite.

8.26 A.M. The dog is evidently in some pain from the bite; he turns round and round in endeavouring to lick the bitten part.

8.29 A.M. Is quieter; pupils normal; no symptom.

8.30 A.M. Able to walk and stand perfectly well.

8.31 A.M. Pupils normal, neither contracted nor dilated: they answer well to light.

8.35 A.M. Slight spasm of diaphragm.

8.36 A.M. Can walk perfectly.

8.39 A.M. Walks with uncertain tread, as if weak; all the legs equally affected.

8.40 A.M. Staggering, but no difference can be observed between the fore and hind legs.

8.41 A.M. Fell over, his fore-legs first giving way; pupils about normal—at any rate, no tendency to dilatation.

8.42 A.M. Lying on his side unable to rise, or even to stand when placed on his legs; all his legs equally weak; twitching of respiratory muscles, also to a less extent of certain muscles in his limbs.

8.43 A.M. Tongue protruded.

8.44 A.M. Pupils contracted; all motion ceased except that of heart.

8.45 A.M. Slight spasm of depressors of larynx.

8.46 A.M. Heart alone acting; pupils suddenly dilated widely.

8.47 A.M. Heart stopped. Dead.

Experiment V.

A large cock had two milligrammes (about ·03 grain) of dried cobra-poison, dissolved in one cubic centimètre of distilled water, injected into its leg.

3.13 P.M. Injection.

3.20 P.M. Respirations 30 per minute.

3.34 P.M. Prefers to sit, but can stand and walk.

3.38 P.M. Head drooping, as if the neck were too weak to support it, but from time to time the head is raised with a jerk.

3.39 P.M. Beak rests on ground.

3.41 P.M. Respirations 25; can barely stand.

3.48 P.M. Respiratory movement very slight.

3.50 P.M. Cannot stand.

3.54 P.M. Cannot keep the eyes open.

3.55 P.M. Respirations 19; pupils somewhat contracted.

4.3 P.M. Respirations 16 ; of a somewhat exaggerated character.

4.5 P.M. Comb has become of a dusky purple colour; slight convulsive movements of body.

4.9 P.M. Respirations 9.

4.13 P.M. Slight convulsions.

4.15 P.M. Pupils contracted ; answer to light.

4.17 P.M. Convulsions.

4.20 to 4.22 P.M. Convulsions continuing, but gradually becoming less violent.

4.25 P.M. Pupils widely dilated. Dead.

Experiment VI.

A medium-sized frog (*Rana tigrina*) had a solution of five centigrammes (·77 grain) of dried cobra-poison, in one cubic centimètre of distilled water, injected into its dorsal sac.

12.42 P.M. Injection.

1 P.M. No change.

1.23 P.M. Struggling violently to escape.

1.40 P.M. Becoming paralysed.

1.53 P.M. Dead.

From these cases it may be gathered that the symptoms of cobra-poisoning are as follow:—

The first manifestation of cobra-poison having been injected beneath the skin is a sensation of pain in the bitten part. It seems to vary much in degree, but is usually described, as in the case given, as being of a stinging and burning character. The site of the wound may also become swollen, red, and painful on pressure. The evidence of the pain occurring in dogs is very clear: the animal often turns round and licks the bitten spot; and if it is the leg that is wounded, it either limps on that leg, or, what is more usual, it draws it up, so as to raise it and relieve it completely of the weight of the body. This action has been termed paralysis of the bitten leg, due to the local contact of the poison with the muscles. Now, though it can be proved that the local effect of cobra-poison on muscle is to weaken it, yet after the bite of a cobra a very small extent of muscle indeed comes in contact with the poison, very often none at all; and if the limb were really paralysed, it would hang uselessly down, dragging upon the ground, instead of being drawn up.

An interval now occurs before the accession of any fresh symptom, but its length varies greatly in different cases. In that of the man quoted it was fifteen minutes; but this is probably considerably under the average time. In another case, related by the same careful observer, an hour and a quarter elapsed in this way; and an intelligent eye-witness, who described a case with great accuracy as to details, stated four hours was passed before any change was noticed. Taking into consideration all the evidence on the subject, it appears probable that in the majority of cases of cobra-bite in the human subject, an interval of an hour occurs before any constitutional symptoms are developed. Under certain exceptional circumstances the symptoms of poisoning may begin almost at once. In the case of dogs bitten by cobras this interval varies very greatly—perhaps fifteen minutes may be taken as its average length, or perhaps a little less.

The retardation of the constitutional symptoms probably means that before cobra-poison can produce any effect, it must be present in the blood in certain proportion, and, of course, in slow absorption, either due to the small quantity of the poison injected, or to its being injected into an unfavourable situation, some time must elapse before this proportion can be attained. In these cases the symptoms are delayed, as is also the fatal result; whereas, should the poison enter the circulation rapidly, as by injection into a vein, the symptoms and fatal result follow immediately. At the same time it is clear that for a short time a fatal quantity of poison may be present in the circulation without producing a symptom; for the bitten part may be sometimes amputated before the occurrence of any sign of poisoning, yet, nevertheless, the animal may die.

In man the first constitutional symptom that cobra-poison produces seems to be a feeling of intoxication, although there appears to be no outward evidence of it. That this symptom is not more frequently described in the history of cases can be easily accounted for by the fact that it would require a certain amount of intelligence on the victim's part to mention it; and in animals, of course, it is impossible to get proof of a purely subjective condition.

The special symptoms of cobra-poison now rapidly manifest themselves. It man it is very commonly observed that the patient cannot any longer keep his eyes open, and about this time it is found that he is losing power in his legs. When he walks he staggers, and, if left unsupported, falls. The arms seem to retain their strength much longer. In the case of dogs, the animal at this stage can scarcely stand without falling frequently, but there does not seem to be that difference between the anterior and posterior extremities that is observed in the legs and arms of a man. Usually, a dog loses strength equally on his fore and hind legs, and rolls from side to side helplessly.

The order in which the symptoms now occur varies in different individuals. In some, loss of the power of speech and of raising the lower jaw is shown, and afterwards profuse salivation; but the salivation may precede. But whichever may occur first, the tongue and the larynx become speedily paralysed; the patient is unable to speak or to clear his throat or to swallow; and the saliva, which is profusely poured forth, trickles down the lips, the patient being no longer able to eject it voluntarily. In dogs it is not unusual for the salivation to be manifested before any other constitutional symptom, and in them a chewing movement of the jaw and lips is often seen immediately before the salivation. Nausea, retching, and vomiting are of frequent occurrence both in men and dogs.

The paralysis now becomes more general and decided. The patient lies on his back, almost incapable of movement. He threatens to be suffocated by the saliva running into his paralysed larynx; should, however, the head be placed on one side, the abundant secretion will flow down his lips. His limbs at this time may be subject to startings and muscular twitchings. His breathing becomes slower and slower, and the respiratory excursus is lessened. He appears to be conscious, but is unable to express himself, through the paralysis of his larynx and tongue; but it is not unfrequently the case for the victim to become quite unconscious. The action of the heart is somewhat quickened, but the organ acts with fair strength. At length the breathing, too slow and too slight to support life, ceases, and with or without general convulsions the heart shortly after stops.

In dogs, as might be expected, convulsions are much more common than in man, being very generally present; and while in man the extinction of the respiratory act is, as a rule, a very slow and gradual process, in dogs it is not unusual for respiration to stop quite suddenly, and almost immediately after for its place to be taken by violent convulsions.

In birds the symptoms are usually very regular in their occurrence. There is the same appearance of local pain. The bird then generally seems drowsy, from its being unable to keep the eyes open, the head droops as if the neck were unable to support it, but the bird constantly recovers itself with a jerk. It at last sinks down to the ground, ultimately falling over on its side, unable to raise either its head or itself. The pupils are, as a rule, somewhat contracted, the eye often watering. The respirations finally become exceedingly slow, and then cease, convulsions and death following. It sometimes happens, as in mammals, that the respiratory centre is almost simultaneously stimulated and paralysed, the bird dying at once.

In the amphibia, there can scarcely be said to be any symptoms of cobra-poisoning; the frog, for instance, only becomes more and more sluggish and paralysed, and is at last found to be dead.

It will be necessary to consider some of the more important conditions in detail, after having noticed the appearances to be found after death.

Post-Mortem Appearances in Cases of Death by Cobra-bite.

Rigor mortis generally comes on about the usual time and is as well marked as it is in death from ordinary causes. The blood in man is fluid, as a rule, and in the lower animals coagulated. If examined directly after death no changes can be recognised by the microscope. After a time the corpuscles may change in shape, become crenated, and blood-crystals may form, but at the moment of death no change can be recognised. The parotid glands may be swollen. The brain presents no marked deviation from normal. The veins of the *pia mater* are usually gorged with blood, and the ventricles often contain turbid fluid. The muscles are often of a dirty red colour. The sub-cutaneous veins bleed freely on section. The lungs may be pale and contain but little blood, but in the human subject they are generally found congested, the bronchi and the smaller tubes being often filled with a thin frothy fluid, and their lining membrane intensely injected. Occasionally portions of food or of remedies are to be found in the air-tubes, the result of administration while the larynx was paralysed. The heart is distended with blood, especially the right side. The liver bleeds freely on incision, and is quite dark from contained blood, but this is not universal. The kidneys vary from normal to excessive congestion, being seen in all stages. The stomach may, or may not, contain food—a proof that cobra-poisoning in the human subject does not always cause evacuation of the contents of the stomach. There is no regular change in the intestinal tract, which may be injected in places. The bladder is generally firmly contracted.

Local Effects of Cobra-poison.

It has been mentioned that severe pain is generally felt in the region of the cobra-bite. There are, however, cases on record which seem to prove that the intense mental shock of snake-bite renders the victim occasionally insensible to the pain. This pain is accompanied by, or rather is dependent upon, a very characteristic local condition, which is of the utmost practical importance. If the body of a man or animal killed by snake-bite be examined, there may be scarcely a sign on the skin to mark the spot where the snake inflicted its bite; or possibly one or two small punctures, or even a scratch, may be found, especially if the part bitten be the fingers, which, of course, are apt to be forcibly and involuntarily retracted when the bite is felt. It may even happen that the part is slightly swollen or discoloured. But whatever may be the condition of the external aspect, there will be found a distinct change in the state of the parts beneath. If an incision be made through the skin and carried through the punctures made by the snake's fangs, very little difference will be found in the true skin. It may be a little more injected than normal, and the punctures will be found to be intensely so just at the edges, and a small quantity of blood may be effused there. But the areolar tissue lying beneath the true skin is the site of the chief change. It will generally be seen to be of a purple colour, and to be infiltrated with a large quantity of coagulable purple blood-like fluid. In addition to this effusion the whole of the neighbouring vessels are intensely injected, which injection gradually fades as the site of the poisoned part is receded from, so that a bright scarlet ring surrounds the purple area, and this in its turn gradually fades into the normal colour of the neighbouring tissue. At the margin, also, the purple blood-like effusion is replaced by a pinkish effusion, which wells out as the incision is made. This effusion of pinkish fluid may often be traced up in the tissues surrounding the vessels which conveyed to the system the poison they had absorbed from the part. In one case, in which the victim was bitten on the hand, the effusion from the veins could be traced as high as the elbow. These are the essential characters of the local effects produced by cobra-bite; but they may vary a good deal in degree, depending, probably, upon the amount of poison injected and the time the subject lived after being bitten. It has been asserted that the nature of these local changes in snake-bite is merely a hæmorrhage into the tissues from vessels that have been divided by the fangs of the snake, with effusion of blood from the vessels around. But though it is true that sometimes a very small amount of blood may be found at the site of the punctures, yet it is clear that this explanation will not account either for the great pain that is felt in the part, or for the intense injection of the neighbouring vessels. To determine the nature of these changes, dissections were made both on the human subject and on the lower animals of individuals that had died of snake-bite; also incisions were made into the tissues at the place where snakes had bitten at various intervals after the bite. The result of these observations is to show that directly after the poison is injected into the tissue its vessels become enlarged and gorged with blood, effusion is poured out immediately; and as the engorgement and stagnation of blood increase the effusion becomes more blood-like, from its containing more of the contents of the vessels. Now, these processes are singularly rapid in occurring. In an animal that only lived thirty seconds after the injection of the poison, a well-marked circle of vascular injection was found at the site of the poison. In another case, in one minute sufficient effusion had been poured out to attract the attention of a casual observer.

Should the animal recover from the constitutional effects of the poison, the result of these local changes will be profuse suppuration and sloughing of the parts in which the poison was deposited. Now, simple effusion of blood is very rarely followed by suppuration. In scurvy and allied diseases, and after injuries, we constantly see effusions of blood rapidly absorbed as recovery proceeds. Again, effusion of blood is seldom attended by pain. Moreover, by using solutions of cobra-poison of different strengths any degree of local mischief can be produced—from an engorgement and acute effusion that scarcely differs from blood, to a slight hyperæmia attended with a pale serous-like effusion.

From these considerations it appears evident that the local effect of cobra-poison is simply severe and acute inflammation, to which the pain attending cobra-bite is due, with a more than ordinary tendency to effusion from the blood-vessels. Corroborative testimony to what is here advanced must be present to the mind of everyone who has had much to do in the manipulation of cobra-poison. A very frequent, but involuntary, experiment is to get some of the poison into the eye. Should the circumstance not be at once noticed, so as to permit the eye being washed out immediately, after a very short time a smarting pain is felt in it; and if it is examined it will be found red and watering, the vessels becoming rapidly enlarged, and, in fact, an acute attack of conjunctivitis with chemosis is set up, which may last for days.

The subject has been specially dwelt on here, as on it can be founded an easy method of deciding whether a person has really been poisoned by a snake. One of the most difficult subjects in connection with snake-bite is to know for certain whether the patient has really been *poisoned* by a snake or not, for it is clear that unless the venomous snake really injects his poison into the victim there is no danger. Now, the mark of the teeth is no guide, or next to none, because a cobra may not leave a single mark visible to the naked eye;

and, on the other hand, fanged harmless snakes, like *Lycodon* and *Dipsas*, may leave punctures in the skin that might easily be mistaken for the wounds caused by the fangs of venomous snakes. And more misguiding, if possible, than any of these, is the victim's description of the snake. From these various causes it often happens that a man is left without an attempt at treatment because the bite is not visible or does not look like that inflicted by a venomous snake, or because there are no symptoms. Now we know that symptoms may not occur till more than an hour has passed, when all chance of preventing the absorption of the poison has gone. On the other hand severe measures have been resorted to, even ending fatally, when it has been proved afterwards that the subject had not been bitten by a poisonous snake at all. It is therefore of great importance to be enabled to say whether a man has really been *poisoned* as well as *bitten* by a snake. This can be done by simply observing the condition of the tissues into which the poison has been injected. No ordinary wounds, not even a poisoned wound such as is received in dissections, can cause the immediate inflammation that is peculiar to snake-poison. In a simple or even ordinary poisoned wound a very considerable time would elapse before any marked change would be noticeable. In the vast majority of cases a simple incision through the skin into the subcutaneous areolar tissue will afford certain information whether the case is one of poisonous snake-bite or not; for even though there may be considerable differences in degree as to the amount of inflammation, yet the existence of any at all must indicate that there must be present a cause beyond the mere mechanical injury.

Action of Cobra-Poison on the Nervous System.

That the chief action of cobra-poison is on the nervous system, there can be no doubt. The exact nature of the action, however, is not so clear. The victim of cobra-poisoning just before death is usually an example of very complete general paralysis. Sir Joseph Fayrer and Dr. Brunton, who have written a most elaborate and valuable series of papers on the nature and physiological action of snake-poison, maintain that though the greater part of the nervous system is affected, yet the terminations of the motor nerves suffer especially, and in a very marked manner. They base their reasoning on the results produced by experiments in which the excitability of two nerves of the same animal is tested, one of which has been subjected to the action of the poison, and the other has been kept from contact with the poisoned blood by the limb to which it is distributed being ligatured, the nerve, however, being kept intact. Under these circumstances a great difference will be found in the electric excitability of the two nerves. These experiments have been repeated, with, however, some modification in the details.

The electric arrangements were as follows:—A constant difference of potentials was maintained by means of a galvanic battery between the terminals of the primary series of coils of a Thomson's Slide Resistance. Two flexible insulated wires, the free ends of which terminated in platinum needles, and were used as the electrodes, were connected, the one to the zero end of the primary series of coils, and the other to the sliding contact of the secondary coils. By suitably moving the sliding contacts, any desired difference of potentials could thus be established between the electrodes.

Experiment VII.

A frog (*Rana tigrina*) was killed mechanically at 12.18 P.M., but reflex action continued for some time afterwards.

1.6 P.M. Muscle was found to be infinitely sensitive. Nerve, stimulated with 0 06 volt, produced distinct contraction; both sides give the same result.

This experiment shows how sensitive muscle and nerve remain for some time after death from purely mechanical causes.

Experiment VIII.

The right thigh of a frog (*Rana tigrina*) was ligatured so as to completely prevent the blood circulating in the part below the ligature. The sciatic nerve was not included in the ligature. One cubic centimetre of solution of cobra-poison, composed of equal parts of distilled water and fresh cobra-poison was injected into its dorsal sac.

2.53 P.M. Injection.

It gradually became paralysed till it ceased to show any signs of reflex action.

3.33 P.M. The muscles of the left or poisoned side contracted with 2·97 volts.

3.33½ P.M. The muscles of the right or non-poisoned side contracted with 2·16 volts.

3.37 P.M. Nerve of poisoned side caused contraction of muscle when stimulated with 2·7 volts.

3.39 P.M. Ligatured (or non-poisoned) nerve, 1·08 volts.

Here there was a marked difference between the poisoned and the non-poisoned side, the non-poisoned side being the more sensitive, but the nerve on the poisoned side had lost its excitability to a greater extent than the muscle. But the paralysis of both the muscle and the nerve was well marked.

Experiment IX.

The right thigh of a frog (*Rana tigrina*) was ligatured with the exception of its sciatic nerve, and one cubic centimetre of cobra-poison solution, consisting of equal parts of distilled water and fresh cobra-poison, injected into its dorsal sac.

12.48½ P.M. Injection.

12.58 P.M. Reflex movement ceased.

1.40 P.M. Muscles of left or poisoned leg contracted with 2.43 volts.

1.40½ P.M. Muscle of right or non-poisoned leg with 1.89 volts.

1.44½ P.M. Nerve on poisoned side caused contraction in muscle when excited by 10·8 volts.

1.46 P.M. Non-poisoned nerve with 0·54 volts.

In this experiment the sensitiveness both of the non-poisoned muscle and nerve, in comparison with that of the poisoned side, was greater than even in the former experiment.

These experiments seem to make it probable that cobra-poison has some special property in deadening the terminations of the motor nerves; and Sir Joseph Fayrer and Dr. Brunton have, in support of this view, given some experiments in which, on irritating the spinal cord with an induced current, contraction was caused in the non-poisoned leg, but not in the poisoned.

The following experiment had for its object to ascertain if the mechanical excitement of the cord could be transmitted through the poisoned nerve.

Experiment X.

A frog (*Rana tigrina*) had 0·5 cubic centimetre of fresh cobra-poison injected into its dorsal sac at 2.12 P.M., the right thigh, with the exception of the sciatic nerve, having been previously ligatured.

2.20 P.M. Very slight reflex movement.

2.45 P.M. Passing a current through the spinal cord, with interruption produced by means of a key, the muscles of both legs distinctly contracted at 0·5 volt.

2.52 P.M. Spinal cord, mechanically stimulated, gave distinct twitchings in both poisoned and non-poisoned legs.

In all these experiments, as long as the cord possessed power at all, contraction could be excited in either leg, provided the nerves had not been mechanically injured, which would rather indicate that the nerves retained their irritability, at the same time that the excitability of the cord was exceedingly quickly lost. Of course a good deal of allowance must be made for the difference in the method of excitation pursued in the two series of experiments. But though the above experiments go to prove that the excitability of the motor nerves lasted as long as that of the spinal cord, yet the difference in the excitability between the two sides in the former experiments showed how powerfully paralysing cobra-poison is. These experiments, then, tend to show that the spinal nervous system is rapidly paralysed by cobra-poison, but that the terminations of the motor nerves only suffer, *pari passû*, with the cord itself, and the poison has no elective affinity for the ends of the nerves. Nor are the results of the experiments of Sir Joseph Fayrer and Dr. Brunton incompatible with this view. For when one thigh of the subject of the experiment was ligatured and the other was poisoned, when the cord was excited by a current the stimulus had to be transmitted to the non-poisoned leg through the trunk of the nerve which was unaffected, whereas on the other leg it had to overcome the resistance induced by the paralysing poison. There is no need to suppose a special effect of the poison on the ends of the motor nerves; the different lengths of the trunks affected would account for a considerable difference. To this we have also to add the paralysing effect on muscle, which, though not so great as on the nerve, is yet not unimportant, and would tell on the same side.

Moreover, it does not necessarily follow that because a nerve to which poison has had access conveys electrical stimuli in a very imperfect manner, or not at all, therefore that the effect of that poison has been to paralyse the nerve. It is unfortunate that the only test we have of the vitality of a nerve is its power of causing contraction in a muscle when irritated by electricity or mechanically. It would be going too far to say, therefore, that because a nerve did not transmit such rude stimuli it was dead; and even if the animal loses the power of withdrawing a limb that is being painfully stimulated, the break in the power of conducting impressions or stimuli may be in any part of the nervous chain necessarily called into requisition in such an action.

A poison that produces death by totally different

means than paralysis, may yet cause in nerves a complete deadness to stimuli.

Experiment XI.

The right thigh of a frog (*Rana tigrina*) was tightly ligatured, so as to completely prevent circulation through the limb, the nerve being included. One cubic centimetre of a solution of strychnia, containing two centigrammes of strychnia, was injected into its dorsal sac.

12.53 P.M. Injection.

12.56 P.M. Tetanus.

1.10 P.M. Reflex action ceased.

1.23 P.M. Muscles of right leg infinitely sensitive.

1.25 P.M. Muscles of left (poisoned) leg contract with 0.75 volt.

1.39 P.M. Right sciatic nerve infinitely sensitive, causes muscular contraction with less than 0·0001 volt.

1.45 P.M. Left sciatic nerve causes contraction with 15 volts.

Now, strychnia certainly does not kill by paralysis, and yet the difference between the poisoned and the non-poisoned sides, in regard to their nerves, was more marked than in cobra-poisoning. In another frog this difference was very pronounced before the strychnia had ceased to produce tetanus, so that it occurs long before exhaustion has taken place. The complete cessation of the vital functions through tetanus is the real cause of death, and the deadening of the nerves is simply the result of the excessive nervous discharges that have taken place through them. Thus, though the trunk or extremity of the nerve may be found paralysed, this does not prove that paralysis was the cause of death, or that it was the direct result of the action of the poison on the nerve.

In this direction another point must be taken into account. One of the most characteristic features of cobra-poisoning in the human subject, is paralysis of the legs. The patient is unable to walk or to stand, though his arms as yet have not experienced any loss of power. Now it would be difficult to suppose that this was due to the terminations of the motor nerves of the legs becoming paralysed, while those of the arms remained unaffected. It is much more probable that the spinal cord is becoming paralysed ; one of the first effects of which would be that it would lose the power of maintaining the tone and necessary contraction in the many complex groups of muscles on which the upright posture is dependent.

But in cobra-poisoning in dogs, paralysis of the hind-legs without the fore, is rarely seen. In the vast majority of cases, power is lost simultaneously in all four mombers. As a rule, in those cases in which it has been noticed that the hind-legs have suffered first, the animal has been bitten on the hind-leg, which would always cause a certain amount of lameness, and difficulty of walking with the hind-quarters, due to the local effect of the poison. But even with this source of fallacy it holds good that in men suffering from cobra-poisoning, paraplegia is a most characteristic symptom; whereas it is exceptional in dogs. Why, then, as a rule, should paraplegia occur in men, and not in dogs? Standing and walking are to a very great extent reflex acts. A man when walking places one foot on the ground, and the sensation of contact with the ground serves as a stimulus to a centre in the cord by which the motor impulse to move the other leg is excited, and paralysis of these few lower centres would at once impair the action. But in dogs the mechanism is very different. They move the fore-leg of one side with the hind-leg of the other. It is necessary, then, that the centres governing the movements in these limbs should be coupled, so to speak, together. The stimulus that moves the fore-leg of the one side, has to excite simultaneous movement in the hind-leg of the other. Therefore, all the inferior, or rather posterior, extremity of the cord has to do in the case of the dog, is merely to transmit the motor impulse from the fore-part; whereas, in man, the inferior part of the cord has to translate a sensation into a stimulus to excite movement. It is, therefore, probable that the earliest injury inflicted by cobra-poison on the nervous system is a paralysis of the centres in the lower part of the cord.

It will have been observed that paralysis of the lips,

tongue, larynx and pharynx, as evinced by inability to retain the saliva within the mouth, by incapacity to move the tongue, or to speak, or to swallow, are very prominent signs of cobra-poisoning both in men and animals. It is singular that the striking resemblance of these symptoms to the disease known as glosso-laryngeal paralysis has not been previously noticed. Now, the preponderance of medical opinion attributes this disease to lesion of certain tracts of the medulla. It cannot be thought, therefore, anything but reasonable to connect both diseases with paralysis of those centres in the medulla oblongata which are so closely associated together, and which are in connexion with the roots of the vagus, the spinal accessory, and the hypo-glossal nerves and the lower nucleus of the facial. But the resemblance does not end here. In both diseases the respiration becomes feebler and feebler, and the victim, at last, dies suffocated. In other words, the lesion in the one case, and the paralysing poison in the other, have invaded the respiratory nucleus so near to the centres they have already destroyed, and have thus rendered the respiratory act difficult, and, at last, impossible. Lastly, after all the lower centres have been completely paralysed, the one by which connection is made with the second, fifth, and seventh nerves still acts, and the eye is closed when touched, and even when approached, after the animal is dependent on artificial respiration for life. For these reasons it seems natural to conclude that the principle action of cobra-poison on the nervous system consists of an extinction of function, extending from below upwards, of the various nerve centres constituting the cerebro-spinal system; and though, no doubt, other parts of the nervous system suffer, it is evident that cobra-poison has a special affinity for acting on the respiratory centre, and those other ganglia allied to it in the medulla oblongata, which are in connection with the vagus, the spinal accessory and the hypo-glossal nerves, and that it is directly to this destructive action that we have to attribute death in most cases of cobra-poisoning.

In very rapid cases of poisoning, when a very large quantity of poison has entered the circulation at once, instead of the gradual extinction of function of the cerebro-spinal centres, the poison appears to act almost immediately by stopping the action of the respiratory centre. There is, of course, no time in these cases to watch the gradual extension of the influence of the poison on the nervous system. It also happens that before cobra-poisoning paralyses the cerebro-spinal centres, it first stimulates them, and produces irregular action. This is sometimes very marked in regard to the respiratory centre, when a large quantity of cobra-poison has entered the circulation with considerable rapidity; and in this case it is very often seen that the other centres in the cord have shared in this stimulation before becoming paralysed; the result being irregular

No. I.—TRACINGS OF RESPIRATORY MOVEMENTS OF A FOWL UNDER GRADUAL COBRA POISONING.

I

Normal Respiration.

II

Slightly exaggerated breathing.

III

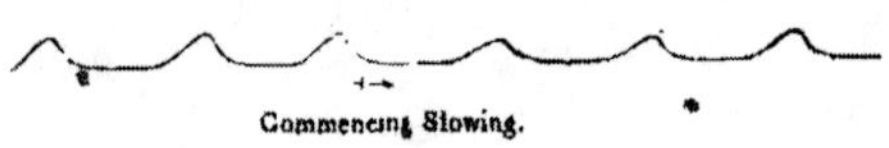

Commencing Slowing.

IV

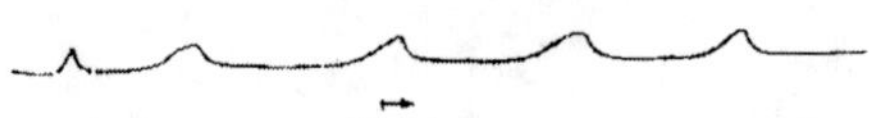

Slowing.

V

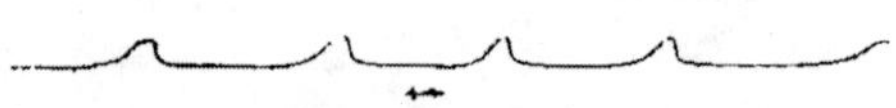

Slowing greater. Sudden and abrupt inspiration and expiration.

VI

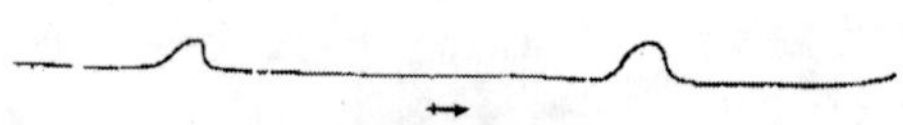

Great slowness.

VII

Respiratory movement barely perceptible.

VIII

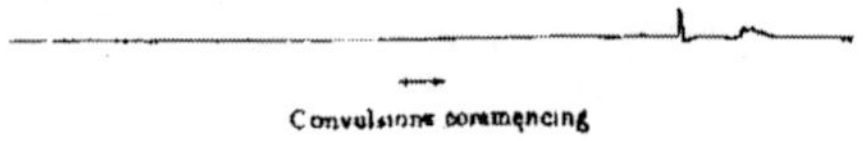

Convulsions commencing

contractions in various groups of muscles. They, however, are not so well marked as those produced by stimulation of the respiratory centre, but they are equally rapidly followed by complete paralysis.

ACTION OF COBRA-POISON ON THE RESPIRATION.

The action of cobra-poison on the respiratory function deserves the closest attention, as death is generally the direct result of the extinction of this function by the effect of the poison.

The first change that is noticed in the breathing of an animal after the introduction of cobra-poison, is a decided quickening and deepening of the respiratory movement. This effect is no longer to be perceived after section of the vagi, and it has been asserted that the acceleration is due to the stimulation of those nerves by the poison. But section of the vagi is always followed by excessive slowing of the respiratory movement; thus, in dogs, the respirations are generally reduced by one-half. It is not improbable, therefore, that an agent that would somewhat stimulate and accelerate the action of the respiratory centre, would fail in producing this result if administered directly after an operation that had so powerfully retarding effect. The inhibitory effect of section of the vagi may be too great to allow of the accelerating action of the poison being perceived. But this quickening, however produced, is merely temporary, and after an interval of uncertain duration the respiration will be found to be slower, and the slowness to increase. The respiratory movement is also lessened in extent. The slowing and lessening of the respiration become at last too great to allow of the blood being properly oxygenated, and, after the usual symptoms characteristic of asphyxiation, the animal dies.

The simplest form in which one can observe the effect of cobra-poison on respiration, is afforded by the common fowl. The stethometric chart marked No. I, gives, in a concise manner, the effects of cobra-poisoning when the action is very gradual. The first line gives the normal respiratory tracing. The main points to be noticed in the succeeding tracings, are the slight quickening first perceived, and the increase of the excursus. These are followed by rapidly increasing retardation, with a certain amount of lessening of the excursus, though the excursus is less affected than the frequency It is also to be noticed that inspiration becomes sudden and abrupt, and is immediately followed by an expiration equally sudden. The movement that remains, therefore, allows no time for that gradual filling and emptying of the air-spaces of the lungs, that would permit a free interchange of air, and is thus necessarily peculiarly unfitted for respiration. In line VI. these characters are well marked, the slowing especially being excessive. A kind of struggle against the poison is to

No II—RESPIRATORY TRACINGS FROM A FOWL THAT DIED VERY RAPIDLY FROM A LARGE DOSE OF COBRA POISON. THE TRACINGS ARE NEARLY CONTINUOUS.

I

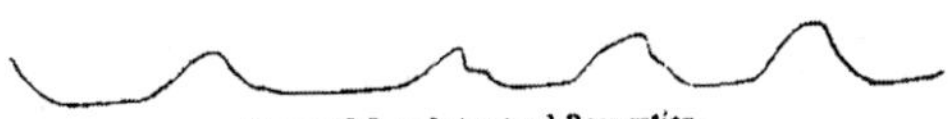

Slow and deep but natural Respiration.

II

Quickened.

III

Still more quickened.

IV

Slightly lessened Excursus.

V

Excursus very slight.

VI

Respiration ceased—Convulsions.

No. III.—TRACINGS OF RESPIRATORY MOVEMENTS OF DOG WITH COBRA POISONING.

I

Normal but deep Respiration.

II

Quickened.

III

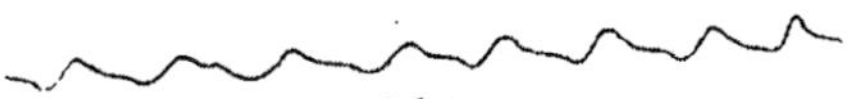

Lessened Excursus.

IV

Movement greatly lessened.

V

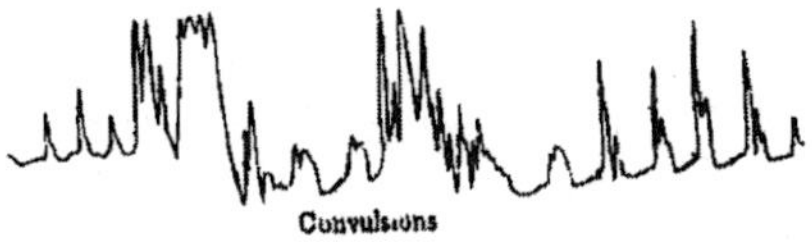

Convulsions

VI

Termination of Convulsions.

be observed in the greater excursus of the movement; probably due to carbonic acid stimulation, but the sudden and jerky character is unabated. In No. VII. the respiratory movement is reduced to a barely perceptible movement of the chest walls, completely incapable of effecting respiration. No. VIII. shows even this movement absent; but at the end of the tracing, the commencement of the convulsions that terminate life is marked. Chart No. II presents some contrasts of interest. It gives nearly the whole course of the respiratory movements of a fowl, from the moment of the injection of the poison till the occurrence of death, in a case in which a large amount of cobra-poison was given, causing death very rapidly. From it will be seen how very much more pronouuced the acceleration is when a large quantity of poison is given, and that when the stage of acceleration is passed the excursus is lessened quite as rapidly as the frequency. The respirations before the administration of the poison bear to the respirations at their greatest degree of acceleration, in the tracing IV., the ratio of four to seven. Chart No. III. is a series of tracings from a large pariah dog, the acceleration followed by retardation, and the accompanying diminution of excursus are well shown; but the nature of the convulsive movements at the end are of great interest. They begin by regular contractions of the respiratory muscles; in the period of their greatest violence they lose all respiratory character, and then gradually fade away in gentler and gentler attempts at inspiration. The cat is an animal that shows a peculiar power of resisting cobra-poison, presenting a marked contrast to the dog. Chart No. IV. is from a cat, in whom this resisting power was prominent. After the retardation of respiration is accomplished, it will be noticed that an occasional deep respiration occurred; it is as if the animal, aware of its lessening breathing power, made conscious efforts to assist respiration. A similar feature appears to have been frequently noticed in the human subject, under like circumstances.

The series of tracings in Chart V. shows graphically the instantly destructive action of cobra-poison on the respiratory function, when a large quantity of the poison suddenly enters the circulation. They are taken from a dog, in whom the following observations were made.

Experiment XII.

A powerful pariah dog had one cubic centimetre of fresh cobra-poison injected into its saphena vein. No change was noticed for thirty seconds; at the end of that time normal respiration abruptly stopped, its place being taken by violent and irregular contractions of the respiratory muscles. The action of the heart continued strong, but increased greatly in frequency. Very soon all movement ceased, with the exception of that of the heart, which continued acting for about ten

No. IV—TRACINGS OF THE RESPIRATORY MOVEMENTS OF A CAT UNDER THE INFLUENCE OF COBRA POISON.

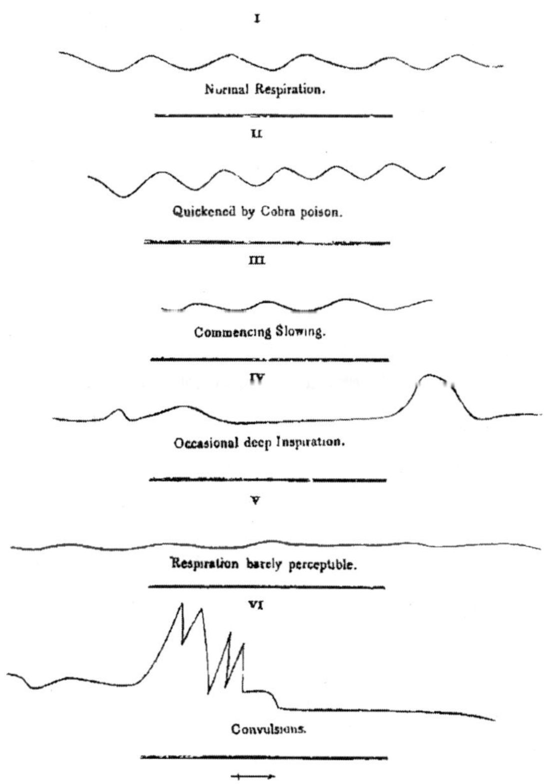

No. V—CONTINUOUS TRACING OF RESPIRATORY MOVEMENTS OF DOG FROM THE MOMENT OF INTRAVENOUS INJECTION OF COBRA POISON TILL DEATH.

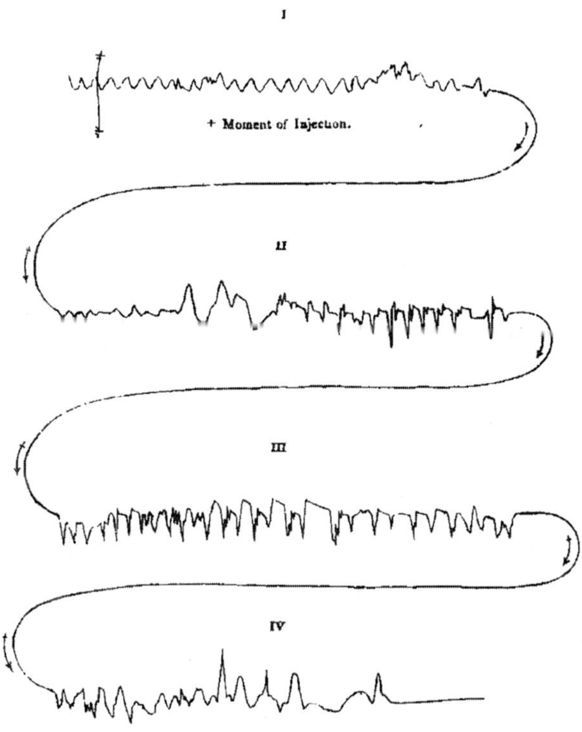

seconds longer. The whole time from injection to death was under 100 seconds.

Chart No. V. is a continuous tracing of the respiration of this animal from the administration of the poison till death. It will be seen that the normal respiratory rhythm is suddenly displaced by violent alternate upheavings and depressions of the chest walls, and that then all movement at once stops. But it will be noticed that the convulsions, though, of course, irregular, have a distinctly respiratory character. When cobra-poison, then, enters the circulation in large quantity, it stimulates the respiratory centre to such a degree that convulsive action of the respiratory muscles is produced, but after a very brief period complete and permanent paralysis of the respiratory apparatus is induced. It is worthy of note that rapid as death in this case was, the action of the heart continued after that of the respiration had ceased.

To sum up the different modes in which cobra-poison destroys the respiratory function :—First, almost instantaneous paralysis of the respiratory centre, a primary stimulation of a very violent but very transient character having occurred. This form of death must be exceedingly rare, if it ever occur, in the human subject, as the shortest period of fatal poisoning in man on record appears to have been a little under a quarter of an hour. Secondly, a more gradual method, the poison having been more slowly absorbed, when no marked change occurs for some time, and then some irregularity in respiration is noticed, and the respiratory action is soon, but, at the same time, gradually abolished; the convulsions of asphyxia may terminate life. This mode of death is very commonly seen in dogs which have been bitten by vigorous cobras. Lastly, there is that gentle primary stimulation of the respiratory function which is shown only by acceleration, and which is soon followed by lessening and retardation of the respiratory movement, and, finally, by its complete cessation. This appears to be the way in which cobra-poison in the vast majority of cases destroys the human subject.

It should be noted that, though the final convulsions of asphyxia which occur in cobra-poisoning can be removed at will by artificial respiration, and that they recur when the aëration of the blood is stopped, yet that the process of natural respiration cannot be restored by these means after it has once ceased, though the action of the heart and life may be prolonged for some time.

Effect of Cobra-poison on the Circulation, Temperature, Special Senses, Secretion, and the Blood.

Cobra-poison cannot be said to exercise a very great effect on the circulation. The heart can be kept acting, and the blood circulating, for very many hours after the rest of the functions of the body have been suspended, if only artificial respiration is continued. In ordinary cases of cobra-poisoning the heart can generally be felt acting for a short time after respiration has stopped. Absorbed in the ordinary way, cobra-poison appears to slightly accelerate the heart's action, and it also lessens the blood-pressure, at any rate for some time. Sir Joseph Fayrer and Dr. Brunton have produced death by tetanizing the heart by injecting cobra-poison into the circulation; but this was done by throwing the poison directly into a very large vessel, as the carotid artery or jugular vein, in a small animal —the guinea-pig.

Cobra-poison also appears to have but little influence on the temperature of the body. Sometimes a very slight rise is to be noticed; generally there is no change, and even a slight fall has been observed. It is probable, therefore, that it has little, if any, effect. The following experiment will show this:—

Experiment XIII.

A healthy pariah dog had a temperature of 102°·9 F. in the rectum. The pulse was 81, and the respirations 34. At 12.45 P.M. it was bitten by a vigorous cobra.

12.48 P.M. Lame in bitten leg, which is drawn up.

1 P.M. Seems quite unaffected.

1.10 P.M. Affected; staggers when it moves.

1.15 P.M. Temperature in rectum 103°·1 F.

1.16 P.M. Pulse 78, pupils normal.

1.17 P.M. Respirations 28.

1.20 P.M. Slight twitchings of respiratory muscles.

1.23 P.M. Respirations 8.

1.24 P.M. Strong convulsions; micturated; pupils contracted.

1.25 P.M. All respiratory movements stopped; temperature 103°·1 F.

1.26 P.M. Pupils dilated.

1.27½ P.M. Heart stopped. Dead.

The temperature began to fall directly after death.

In cases of cobra-poisoning of longer duration, we have the disturbing influence of the local inflammation to consider, which would account for some variation in temperature.

In the special senses and their organs no marked change can be seen in cobra-poisoning: as long as consciousness is preserved the victim appears to see and hear perfectly. In regard to the eye there is very little to be noticed. The pupil can be said neither to be dilated nor contracted by the influence of the poison; at the moment of death it dilates widely, while up to that time it responds to light. If life be preserved by artificial respiration the pupils remain somewhat contracted. I once noticed the pupil remain contracted after death from cobra-poisoning, in which long-continued artificial respiration had been resorted to. Whether cobra-poisoning affects accommodation cannot well be known, and what evidence there is appears to be against its being affected. The eye retains its sensitiveness, and the eye-lid the power of closing, for some time after most other parts are paralysed. But in the human subject drooping of the upper eye-lid is often an early symptom of the action of the poison.

On secretion cobra-poison appears to have considerable influence. It seems as if most secreting structures were stimulated by it. The lachrymal glands act freely during cobra-poisoning. Salivation is a most marked and constant symptom; it is very rarely, indeed, absent in dogs, and it appears to be equally common in man. In dogs, the saliva often runs from the mouth literally in streams; nor in man does it seem much less copious. Should only a small quantity of poison have entered the system, salivation may be the only symptom. The whole of the mucous tract is also apparently in an active state of secretion. After the stomach has been thoroughly emptied by vomiting, the animal will often bring up repeatedly large quantities of mucus, and mucous discharges are also frequently evacuated from the rectum. The respiratory mucous membrane, too, participates. Mucous secretion sometimes flows from the nose, and the air-tubes are not unusually found bathed in fluid. Of its action on the liver and kidneys it is very difficult to get evidence, as the time before death is generally so short; in the more chronic cases sometimes the kidneys appear to act very freely, but sometimes there is a diminution of urine.

There is but little evidence of the effect of cobra-poisoning on the blood. It is, of course, by the blood acting as carrier that the poison is able to reach the system, and the blood of a cobra-poisoned animal is poisonous, also, to another animal. It is clear, therefore, that the poison exists in the blood. That it causes changes in it, there is also evidence. In a man poisoned by a cobra it is very generally, indeed, found that his blood has become incoagulable, though in dogs it is exceptional for this to be the case. Very occasionally, too, the mucous discharges from the body are stained with blood, as if the relation existing between the blood and the tissues had been in some way altered. If, however, the experiments given at the commencement are referred to, it will be seen that in not one was there noted a discharge of blood from a mucous orifice, and they were selected on account of being typical. Still, there are cases on record which prove that discharges of blood, though rare, occasionally occur, perhaps through individual peculiarities.

The interval that occurs between the injection of the poison and the development of the symptoms is, to a certain extent, evidence of blood-change, as the pause can be proved to depend on two factors. The one factor is the time required for the absorption of the poison, for it is lessened by the poison being injected simultaneously into several different sites, or into a spot where absorption is very active. The other is clearly dependent on some secondary change produced by the poison, probably in the blood, for which time is necessary; for if the part into which the poison has been injected be excised before the occurrence of a single constitutional symptom, yet, nevertheless, the animal may die apparently as rapidly as if no interference had been attempted, showing that the mere presence of the poison in the blood, even in sufficient quantity to kill, is not capable of producing directly a physiological effect. On the other hand, to prevent grave misconception, it should be stated that it is quite possible to save life by excision of the bitten part, if it be done sufficiently quickly to prevent any material absorption.

But that the changes in the blood are not considerable there is abundant evidence. Thus, when an animal has survived the nerve symptoms produced by cobra-poison, it at once passes into a state of complete health, and to suffer no further inconvenience from blood-poisoning or other causes, save the local inflammation produced by the bite. The evidence of this, in the following experiment, is very conclusive :—

Experiment XIV.

A large pariah dog had five milligrammes ($\frac{7}{100}$ of a gram) of dried cobra-poison dissolved in 0·3 cubic centimetre of distilled water injected into its hind-leg.

12.12 P.M. Injection.

4 P.M. Vomited; no other symptom.

7.30 P.M. Salivated; depressed.

10.15 P.M. Still depressed; salivation slight; respirations 14 per minute.

12.5 A.M. Still salivated; very depressed.

8 A.M. Very weak, hardly able to walk; all the legs equally affected.

8.25 A.M. Respirations 12; pupils somewhat dilated, but contract to light. Site of injection very red, hot, and swollen.

11.30 A.M. Respirations 15; frothy salivation.

12 P.M. Rectal temperature 39° C.

12.38 P.M. Pulse about 120, extremely irregular; chewing movement of jaw and lips; salivation considerable.

2.21 P.M. Better; can walk; salivation ceased; ate sparingly.

7.30 P.M. Recovering fast; urinated, no albumen in urine.

8 A.M. Seems quite well; purulent discharge from site of injection; respirations 20; pulse 120.

The dog was kept under observation, and remained quite well. The normal pulse rate was 90, and respirations 28.

Here, though the most severe nerve symptoms were present, they completely passed off, leaving the animal at once in a state of convalescence. There was no trace either of permanent nerve injury or of blood poisoning.

The same also occurs in the human subject. I am indebted to Dr. Richards for the following account of a most interesting case which came under his own observation :—

A man named Bámon Dás, aged forty years, was bitten by a snake ou the shoulder about 3 o'clock in the morning. From his description it was probably the snake termed by the natives of Bengal the "Tentuliah Karís" (a spectacled cobra) about four feet long. He had complained, after the bite, of feeling intoxicated, had vomited, and could neither stand nor speak, though he had continued to be perfectly conscious. At 10 A.M., when Dr. Richards saw him, he was being supported in the sitting posture by two men. Near the posterior border of the deltoid of the left arm were two rather indistinct fang-marks at some considerable distance from each other; one fang-mark, however, more resembled a scratch than a puncture. The arm was painful, hot, and swollen, measuring eleven inches in circumference, whereas the other arm at a similar part measured only nine and a half. On cutting through the punctures the track of the fang was clearly visible, though the staining of the areolar tissue was very slight indeed. He had no power whatever over the eye-lids, which had dropped, leaving only the lower parts of the pupils visible. The pupils were perfectly natural, and the irides responded. When asked to identify people he pushed his head back so as to bring the person into the line of vision. He could, in fact, see perfectly well. The hearing was not affected. There was profuse salivation, the saliva streaming down from the corner of his mouth. The lower lip had drooped. He could speak but very indistinctly, so indistinctly that his friends had to ask him to repeat what he said. The intonation was peculiarly nasal, much resembling that of persons who have lost part of their palate. The lips were not used in his endeavour to pronounce his name, consequently the labial *b* was omitted, and he answered with a very indistinct and nasal "Aon Dás." On attempting to swallow some water it was returned through the nostrils. He was unable to clear his throat, which caused him some distress. He felt some difficulty in breathing, though the respiration was but slightly embarrassed. The superficial temporal and frontal veins were very distinct and tortuous, being gorged with blood. He could not walk himself, but if supported walked with an unsteady gait, though he had perfect control over his upper extremities. Still felt intoxicated and his body hot. Pulse 96, full and strong. Temperature 100°·5 F. Occasional retching.

11.30 A.M. Slightly better; still feels intoxicated; temperature 101° 1 F.

1 P.M. Temperature 101°·5 F.

2.30 P.M. Arm a little more swollen—now measures

eleven inches and a half; has passed a large quantity of urine.

Feels a little sick, and the veins about the face are still rather gorged. Now speaks distinctly, and can swallow. Suffering rather severely from the pain in the arm.

From this time the arm got gradually better, and the man completely recovered.

In this case we have an example of severe cobra-poisoning, well described, in which the nerve symptoms were fully developed, and yet, when they had passed away, the man was at once in a state of thorough and complete recovery.

In the published report of the Snake Commission, by Drs. Ewart, Richards and Mackenzie, in the experiments given as to the least amount of poison required to kill, no animal died after thirty-two hours; and the one case that lived that time, it is clear from the history, died of nerve affection. Of the rest that survived, though many of them had the most serious nerve symptoms, not one appears to have given any evidence of blood alteration. The microscope, also, gives no evidence of structural change in the blood. In cobra-poisoning, also, albumen in the urine is unknown. In animals that have suffered most severely from nerve symptoms, in which I have tested the urine, albumen has not been present in a single instance, either in fatal or non-fatal cases. When, however, artificial respiration has been performed for some time, it is not unusual for blood to be present in the urine; but if the kidneys be examined in these cases the wonder will be, not that blood was found in the urine, but that any urine was secreted at all to mix with the blood, so great is the renal congestion. This circumstance, therefore, can hardly be taken as evidence of blood change.

In spite, then, of occasional discharges of blood from mucous surfaces, and that the blood of man is generally found fluid after death, if we take into consideration the facts that death, except from nerve symptoms, is unrecorded; that after the subject has recovered from the nerve effects, he at once regains his usual health, sequelæ being unknown, at least if we trust the available evidence—always excepting the local results of cobra-bite which are most severe; and that in the vast majority of cases there is no symptom of serious blood-poisoning even during the occurrence of the nerve symptoms; also that the kidneys give no evidence of altered relation to the blood; and that, as a rule, the coagulability of the blood is not destroyed in animals: we may conclude that though cobra-venom is a nerve poison of surpassing deadliness, as a blood poison it is not an agent of much power.

CHAPTER II.

THE PHYSIOLOGICAL EFFECTS OF THE POISON OF RUSSELL'S VIPER (DABOIA RUSSELLII).

THE snake that it will be most advantageous, for various reasons, to consider next is the *Daboia Russellii*, an extremely poisonous snake, found in great abundance in Bengal proper, in many other parts of India, and in Ceylon. It is a very fierce snake, striking after a little provocation with deadly precision. It has a very stridulous noisy hiss. It belongs to the viperine family of snakes, of which it is a typical member. For this reason it is taken here as an example of a viperine snake in the same way that the cobra was taken as the representative of the colubrine family. It will be best to follow the same plan that was adopted in cobra-poisoning, detailing first the symptoms of a sufficient number of cases of daboia-poisoning to elicit all the points of importance, and then to discuss the conditions on which the fatal results depend. There does not appear to be a well-recorded case of daboia-poisoning in the human subject, so it will be necessary to resort to experiment.

Experiment I.

A small quantity of fresh daboia-poison (about 0·1 cubic centimetre) was injected into the thigh of a pariah dog.

12.20 P.M. Injection.

12.25 P.M. Very lame in the leg in which injection was made.

12.44 P.M. Looks very depressed and sleepy.

12.49 P.M. Slimy motion passed.

12.52 P.M. Very drowsy; unsteady in walking.

12.54 P.M. Pupils widely dilated; iris only just visible.

12.56 P.M. Moaning; lying down with head resting on ground; trying every now and then to stand up, but soon desisting from the attempt.

12.58 P.M. Constantly attempting to rise.

1 P.M. Panting; managed to raise himself to a standing posture; but his legs "doubled up," as it were, under him, and he fell to the ground.

1.5 P.M. Violent respiratory movements; respirations 28.

1.6 P.M. Still able to move his head freely.

1.15 P.M. Still tries occasionally to rise.

1.17 P.M. Moaning.

1.20 P.M. Moderately loud screams.

1.25 P.M. Convulsions.

1.32 P.M. Convulsions.

1.34 P.M. Dead.

Experiment II.

A pariah dog was bitten in the thigh by a daboia.

11.57 A.M. Bitten.

11.59 A.M. Lame in the bitten leg.

12.3 P.M. Violent convulsions, all the limbs forcibly extended and tense; pupils normal; urinated; screaming.

12.5 P.M. No trace of the convulsions left.

12.8 P.M. Hind-legs paralysed.

12.9 P.M. Vomiting.

12.13 P.M. Screaming.

12.14 P.M. Pupils dilated; not able to stand; much less power in hind than in fore legs.

12 19 P.M. Sanious fluid oozing from rectum.

12.20 P.M Screaming; tongue has a slight tendency to fall to the side of the mouth.

12.21 P.M. Forcible contraction of diaphragm.

12.25 P.M. Respirations 52.

12.30 P.M. Large quantity of blood-coloured fluid passing from rectum.

12 35 P M. Lying down quite paralysed.

12.40 P.M. Respirations rapidly diminishing in number and extent of movement.

12.47 P.M. Respirations about 10 a minute.

12.50 P.M. Respirations reduced to an occasional spasm of inspiratory muscles.

12.55 P.M. Dead.

Experiment III.

A pariah dog had five milligrammes ($\frac{7}{100}$ of a grain) of dried daboia poison injected subcutaneously, dissolved in one cubic centimetre of water.

12.56 P.M. Injection.

1.54 P.M. Quite well; respirations 44.

7 P.M. Ate a good dinner of meat.

11 P.M. Seems a trifle depressed; has had copious motions, but quite natural.

3 A.M. No change.

6 A.M. Looks a good deal depressed; respirations 48 a minute.

7.30 A.M. Pupils contracted; panting; respirations 60 a minute.

8.15 A.M. Panting excessively.

8.30 A.M. Passed a sanious motion.

8.45 A.M. Respirations 80; excessive dyspnœa; blood oozing from mouth.

9.30 A.M. Dead.

After death the fatal dyspnœa was found to be dependent on œdema of the lungs.

Experiment IV.

A small pariah dog was bitten in the thigh by a small *Daboia Russellii.*

12.34 P.M. Bitten.

12.35 P.M. Slightly panting.

12.35½ P.M. Fell over suddenly in violent convulsions, his hind-legs being especially strongly convulsed; pupils contracted.

12.36 P.M. Slight attempts at respiration.

12.39 P.M. Dead.

Experiment V.

A somewhat small pariah had a pulse of 88; respirations 30; rectal temperature 102°·2 F. (39° C.)

3.24 P.M. Bitten by a *Daboia Russellii* in the thigh; struggled and cried much while being bitten.

3.25 P.M. Lame, draws up the leg that was bitten.

3.28 P.M. General muscular spasm of the most violent character, all parts of the body taking part. The animal fell down, and rolled in convulsions; even the muscles of the eye-balls shared in the spasms, jerking the eyes about in the strangest way.

3.30 P.M. Convulsions ceased; complete paralysis of both hind-legs; tries to stand, but cannot get beyond just resting on his fore-legs.

3.31½ P.M. Spasms of muscles of eye-ball continue; respirations very shallow, 68; pupils somewhat dilated.

3.37 P.M. Muscles of eye-ball at rest; seems utterly prostrate, and unable to move; respirations 40, chiefly abdominal.

3.40 P.M. Respirations 56, shallow; occasionally a deep sigh.

3.44 P.M. Pupils somewhat dilated, but contract to light.

3.47 P.M. Respirations 67, about every tenth one is very deep.

3.50 P.M. Moaning.

3.53 P.M. Pulse 156.

3.55 P.M. Pupils dilated.

3.56 P.M. Moaning: temperature 103°·1 F.

4.1 P.M. Respirations 32; sighing and moaning; lying down paralysed; sanious discharge from rectum; pupils widely dilated.

4.6 P.M. Still moaning.

4.9 P.M. Respirations 36.

4.12 P.M. Respiration reduced to a quick inspiratory spasm, followed by relaxation.

4.15 P.M. Respirations 16.

4.17 P.M. Dead; temperature 103° F.

Experiment VI.

A pariah dog was bitten on the shoulder by a daboia.

3.7 P.M. Bitten.

3.9 P.M. As the snake had been in captivity some time, the dog was bitten by another daboia.

3.13 P.M. Defecated.

3.14 P.M. Violent spasms of all the limbs, especially the hind ones; arching of back, twitching of muscles of eye-ball; pupils normal; fell over on his side.

3.15 P.M. Pupils dilated.

3.16 P.M. Defecating.

3.18 P.M. Able to get up again; walked about.

3.19 P.M. Lay down again voluntarily.

3.23 P.M. Moaning.

3.37 P.M. Still lying down; is now unable to raise himself, or to stand when raised.

3.41 P.M. Blood-stained motion.

4.3 P.M. Screaming.

4.17 P.M. Respiration failing.

4.30 P.M. Respiration stopped; heart ceased directly afterwards.

From these experiments it will be seen how very great is the dissimilarity of the symptoms in different cases of daboia-poisoning. Hardly any two cases are alike. Thus, in Experiment I., the dog becomes gradually paralysed, and dies of asphyxia. In Experiment II. six minutes after being bitten it falls into severe convulsions, after which it is found to be paralysed, the paralysis ultimately stopping respiration. In Experiment III. no change was observed for seventeen hours, and then the animal died of lung complication. In Experiment IV. in a minute and a half after being bitten, the dog fell over in violent convulsions, and died at once. In Experiment V. three minutes after being bitten the dog had the most violent convulsions, to which paralysis immediately succeeded, which became more and more complete till death. In Experiment VI. there were convulsions, but they passed off, leaving the animal apparently unaffected and able to walk about; then it became gradually paralysed, and in this state died.

We have here nearly every kind of death, from that produced instantly by violent convulsions, to a lung affection coming on many hours after the administration of the poison, and unaccompanied by any nerve symptoms at all.

The following experiments throw some light on the causes of these differences:—

Experiment VII.

A pariah pup had about 0·1 cubic centimetre of fresh daboia poison injected subcutaneously into the shoulder.

12.52 P.M. Injection.

1.0 P.M. Vomiting.

1.1 P.M. Sat down voluntarily.

1.3 P.M. Can stand and walk; defecating.

1.4 P.M. Can stand, but cannot walk.

1.5 P.M. Got up of his own accord to vomit.

1.6 P.M. Can stand, but prefers lying down; pupils contracted.

1.8 P.M. Cannot stand; moaning.

1.11 P.M. Slight sanious discharge from rectum.

1.15 P.M. Short rapid respiration, with an occasional deep inspiration.

1.18 P.M. Pupils contracted.

1.30 P.M. Respiration very slight.

1.38 P.M. Respiration still fainter.

2.6 P.M. Dead.

Experiment VIII.

A pariah pup of the same litter as the one in the last experiment, and as nearly as possible of the same size, had 0·3 cubic centimetre of fresh daboia-poison injected into its shoulder subcutaneously.

1.31 P.M. Injection.

1.32 P.M. Seems in pain.

1.34 P.M. Defecating.

1.35 P.M. Fell over in convulsions.

1.37 P.M. Unable to stand.

1.45 P.M. Lying down; is quite paralysed, but occasionally groans.

2.1 P.M. Totally unconscious.

2.16 P.M. Respiration failing.

2.29 P.M. Dead.

In these two dogs, which were of the same age and size, the daboia-poison was injected into exactly the corresponding part in each, and subcutaneously; but in the latter experiment three times as much poison was injected as in the former case. This was the only difference in the two experiments, and the result was that the animal which had the larger quantity of daboia-poison in four minutes had violent convulsions, and from that time was quite paralysed, whilst the other only gradually became paralysed, and had no symptoms of convulsions at all. The amount of poison given in even the latter case was not above a third of the quantity that a daboia could inject. The poison, in both cases, was from the same viper, and extracted at the same place.

Experiment IX.

A fowl had two centigrammes (about 0·3 grain) of dried daboia-poison, dissolved in 0·3 centimetre of water, injected subcutaneously into its leg.

12.17 P.M Injection.

12.19 P.M. Defecated.

12.20 P M. Twitchings of the muscles of the neck, followed immediately by violent convulsions and death.

Experiment X.

A third of a cubic centimetre of water containing in solution about half a milligramme of dried daboia-poison was injected into the leg of a fowl subcutaneously.

3.37 P.M. Injection.

3.45 P.M. No symptom.

3.52 P.M. Greatly exaggerated respiratory movement.

3.55 P.M. Head drooping, beak resting on ground.

3.59 P.M. Cannot stand.

4.4 P.M. Lying on its side.

4.24 P.M. Convulsions.

4.25 P.M. Dead.

In these two experiments, also, the same thing is to be noticed. Two centigrammes produced the most violent and fatal convulsions, and the result would have been the same if two milligrammes only had been used; whereas half a milligramme produced only the symptoms of paralysis, followed by asphyxia. The convulsions in this case followed the paralysis, and were dependent on asphyxia, precisely in the same way as they occur in cobra-poisoning. From these experiments we see that though a very small quantity of daboia-poison may only cause gradual paralysis, a somewhat larger one will produce death at once by convulsions in an animal of the same size. In the same way it can be proved that the same amount of daboia-poison given to two animals of different sizes, though the larger may escape the convulsions altogether, the smaller may die at once in them.

We must conclude, then, that in daboia-poison we have to do with a substance capable of producing the most violent convulsions, and that the larger the animal the greater is the quantity required to produce this effect. But the convulsions are in no way dependent upon the entrance of the poison directly into a vein, as sometimes happens in the case of cobra-poison; and birds are so susceptible to this substance, that it is only with difficulty that a sufficiently weak solution can be prepared to cause any symptoms at all with the avoidance of convulsions. The first symptom, then, after the local pain, which appears to be peculiarly severe in daboia-poisoning, will very probably be the appearance of convulsions. But their occurrence depends, as we have seen, upon the size of the animal and the amount of poison injected. I have seen an extremely large pariah dog so severely convulsed that it seemed probable that he would die in them. At the same time, a small dog may escape them altogether. It is entirely dependent on the quantity of poison injected by the snake.

If the convulsions occur, they generally take place in from one to ten minutes after the infliction of the bite—probably five minutes is about the average; and they may have any degree of severity, from violent contractions of nearly every muscle in the body, so that the animal dies almost instantaneously, to just a few twitchings of the muscles of the legs or other parts. As a rule, they are severe; every muscle, it seems, taking part in them; the muscles of the eye-balls, even, rolling the eyes about in a most striking manner.

In this state the animal may die at once, as in Experiment IV., or respiration may be established again, only to cease shortly after, the animal remaining completely paralysed in the interval; or the animal may recover consciousness, but remain paralysed, the respiration gradually ceasing, as in Experiment V.; or after the convulsions he may quite recover and show no symptom whatever, but a greater or less interval having occurred, paralysis begins to be manifest, as in Experiment VI. Even when convulsions are absent, marked twitchings of the muscles of the eye, or the neck, or the hind-legs, which completely pass off, may be noticed about five or ten minutes after the bite.

Supposing convulsions to have occurred, the animal will either be found to be completely paralysed, or will ultimately become so. It is occasionally, though by no means universally, noticed that there is a greater loss of power in the hind-legs than in the fore, which is probably due to the exhaustion produced by the violent nervous discharges, which are often particularly severe in the hind-legs. Respiration, directly after the convulsions, may be quite absent; it re-commences generally slowly at first, and then becomes very rapid. The pupils are, after the convulsions, widely dilated, though after a time they may begin to contract again. The respirations, too, ultimately become slower, and the paralysis more profound. Sanious discharges take place from the rectum and other orifices, and finally respiration stops.

Should convulsions not take place, the history is that of advancing paralysis. The respirations and pulse become very greatly accelerated, and there is gradual loss of power in all the limbs; vomiting may occur. Sanious discharges are observed issuing from the rectum, or other parts. The pupils are usually widely dilated; the respirations then become less and less, and may cease with or without convulsions. This is seen in Experiment 1.

But there is a third form of death from daboia-poisoning; it occurs in those cases in which but a small quantity of daboia-poison has been injected. The animal has very few nervous symptoms, very likely none at all; but on the second day it appears ill, refuses food, has diarrhœa, the urine contains albumen, and it may linger on thus for days, ultimately dying exhausted; or some acute complication may supervene, as in Experiment III., causing death rapidly.

In birds, the symptoms following daboia-bite show no variation. The bird is almost at once seized with convulsions, and falls dead.

Experiment XI.

11.30 A.M. A fowl was bitten by a daboia.

11.30¼ A.M. Respirations slightly accelerated.

11.30½ A.M. Violent convulsions.

11.31¼ A.M. Dead.

Birds are most easily affected in this manner by the poison; after them come the Lacertilia.

Experiment XII.

About ·4 cubic centimetre of fresh daboia-poison was injected beneath the skin of a lizard (the *Calotes versicolor*). The respirations were 54 per minute.

3.49 P.M. Injection.

3.51 P.M. Convulsions.

3.52 P.M. Quite paralysed.

3.53 P.M. Respirations 12 per minute.

3.59 P.M. Dead.

Mammals, as it has been stated, are very easily affected by the convulsion-producing agent; but amphibia only have symptoms of gradual paralysis.

Experiment XIII.

A medium-sized frog (*Rana tigrina*) had one centigramme of dried cobra-poison in solution injected into its dorsal sac.

1.12 P.M. Injection.

4.40 P.M. Violent respiratory efforts.

4.39 P.M. Becoming paralysed.

4.53 P.M. Paralysed.

5.11 P.M. Dead.

It is important to notice this difference of power in producing a fatal result in different classes of animals by these two poisons.

Experiment XIV.

Five centigrammes (·77 grain) of dried cobra-poison dissolved in water, were injected into the dorsal sac of a frog (*Rana tigrina*).

12.43 P.M. Injection.

1.40 P.M. Paralysed.

1.50 P.M. Dead.

Experiment XV.

Five centigrammes (·77 grain) of dried daboia-poison, dissolved in water, were injected into the dorsal sac of a frog (*Rana tigrina*), of the same size as the one in the last experiment.

11.38 A.M. Injection.

1.8 P.M. Weak, but struggles occasionally.

2.12 P.M. Some water discharged from nostrils.

2.30 P.M. Lying down extended.

5 P.M. Better; able to move.

8 A.M. Is apparently quite well.

It remained perfectly well.

Thus, while five centigrammes of cobra-poison will kill a frog in seventy minutes, yet the same quantity of daboia-poison will only produce comparatively trifling symptoms, and complete recovery will ensue.

Local Effects of Daboia-bite.

As to the local mischief caused by the bite of the daboia, what has been said about the cobra might be repeated here. But there are one or two points of difference which are of sufficient interest to be mentioned. The fangs of the daboia, being much longer than those of the cobra, produce a much larger and deeper wound. From this it happens that it is much more usual to find blood from divided vessels in daboia-bite than in cobra-bite. The local action is also greater, the pain of daboia-bite appearing to be peculiarly severe. The same acute inflammatory effusion can be found in the daboia-bite, but it has much more the appearance of blood than that found in cobra-bite; a circumstance that is due to the greater power daboia-poison has in causing the contents of the blood-vessels to transude through their walls. However, if a dissection of a daboia-bite be made about three minutes after its infliction, a circle of injected vessels with a pinkish effusion within the meshes of the areolar tissue will be found, sufficient to show the real nature of the process that is commencing. The presence, however, of daboia-poison imparts, so to speak, a "specific" character to the inflammation in the large amount of blood-material in the effusion. The characteristic changes are quite as rapid in occurring as in cobra-bite; if, indeed, they are not more so, and they are of precisely the same nature, the only difference being in regard to degree. They are invariably followed, should the animal live, with sloughing and suppuration, and are equally valuable as evidence of poisoning with those of cobra-bite.

Action of Daboia-Poison on the Nervous System.

Enough has already been said to show that there are considerable differences in the action of daboia and cobra-poisons on the nervous system. Daboia-poison commences its action by producing convulsions. It is true that the animal may escape them, through an insufficient quantity of poison being injected. Now, these convulsions in no way depend upon a large quantity of poison being directly injected into a vein, as in cobra-poisoning, nor are they necessarily immediately followed by paralysis and death, being not mere precursors of the extinction of function of the nerve-centres; but they may, on the contrary, be for the time perfectly recovered from (see Experiment VI.), sometimes an interval of half an hour of perfect health elapsing.

The following experiments show the contrast between the two poisons very well.

Experiment XVI.

One centigramme (·154 grain) of dried daboia-poison was dissolved in one cubic centimetre of distilled water, and the solution was injected, with great care, just beneath the skin of the leg of a fowl.

3.10 P.M. Injection.

3.11 P.M. Slightly lame in the leg in which the injection was made.

3.12 P.M. Violent convulsions.

3.12¾ P.M. Dead.

Experiment XVII.

The same quantity of dried cobra-poison dissolved in the same quantity of water (namely, one centigramme in one cubic centimetre), as in the last experiment, was injected just beneath the skin of the leg of a fowl.

3.30 P.M. Injection.

3.32 P.M. Lying down.

3.34 P.M. Drowsy.

3.35 P.M. Head drooping.

3.36 P.M. Beak resting on ground; unable to stand; eyelids closed; pupils contracted.

3.37 P.M. Unable to lift head from ground.

3.40 P.M. Convulsions; eyes watering.

3.42 P.M. Dead.

Now, in these two experiments the greatest care was taken to ensure the conditions being exactly the same, as regards the amount of poison, the quantity of fluid, and the exact spot into which it was injected. Moreover, to avoid accidental sources of fallacy, the experiment was repeated, with the unfailing result that with daboia-poison the subject of the experiment died at once in convulsions; while in cobra-poisoning the bird went through the course of gradual paralysis, and after respiration was extinguished had the convulsions of asphyxia and died.

These convulsions, therefore, are in no way due to the injection of the poison into a vein, or to the slight stimulation of nerve centres that is seen in cobra-poisoning immediately before paralysis. The next question is, are these convulsions in any way dependent on asphyxia, like those met with in cobra-poisoning, when the poison has been absorbed in the usual way? If the tracings Series No. 6 be examined, some evidence on the subject will be obtained. It is a continuous tracing taken from a fowl that died from daboia-poisoning. In the first line no change will be perceived, in the second line the breathing becomes slightly exaggerated, and then instantly, at the spot marked thus (*), the convulsions begin, and do not cease till death. Respiration was perfectly well performed up to the moment of the invasion of the convulsions, which, therefore, could not have been due to asphyxia.

But the following experiment is still more conclusive on this point.

Experiment XVIII.

A fowl had its trachea opened, and a tube in connection with a bellows, for artificial respiration, inserted into it. A solution, containing two centigrammes (·3 grain) of dried daboia-poison, was then injected subcutaneously into its leg. Immediately on the injection being completed, artificial respiration was commenced.

2.23 P.M. Injection.

2.23½ P.M. Artificial respiration begun.

2.26 P.M. Convulsions in which the bird died.

Here, though ample means were employed to keep the blood oxygenated, the bird died immediately in convulsions. It is clear, therefore, that these convulsions are *primary*, and in no way due to defective aëration of the blood, like those usual in cobra-poisoning. The convulsions are generally very violent, the muscles usually being powerfully contracted, and then relaxation takes place. Sometimes they may remain tense for some time, but they are commonly clonic. They are very general in character, even to the muscles of the orbit. Sometimes they appear to be tonic, the muscles, as it were, clasping forcibly the frame of the victim.

Dr. Weir Mitchell, in investigating the action of the poison of the crotalus or rattle-snake, describes what he terms a "fremitus," or trembling of the muscular fibrils, dependent upon the contact of the poison with the muscle. The following experiment was made, in order to ascertain whether the convulsions were due to this direct action of the poison on the muscles or not.

Experiment XIX.

A fowl was placed under the influence of chloroform, and its right crural nerve divided; the left crural nerve was then isolated, and a ligature placed round all the other structures, so as completely to obstruct the circulation, but the nerve was left uninjured. A small quantity of solution of daboia-poison was subcutaneously injected into the tissues at the back of the neck. Almost directly after, convulsions occurred; but in these convulsions the muscles supplied by the right, or divided nerve, took no part, remaining perfectly flaccid, while the muscles of the left leg were violently tetanized. Here the muscles of the right leg, which were freely supplied with poisoned blood, but the nerve to which was divided, escaped the convulsions, while those of the left leg, which had no contact with the poisoned blood, but whose nerve was still in communication with the central nervous system, took part in them.

It is evident, therefore, that the convulsions depend upon the direct irritation of the central nervous system by the poison, and in no way on the contact of the poison with the muscles. It has also been proved that these convulsions do not depend upon paralysis of the respiratory centre, for they may pass off leaving the animal without a symptom. Though it is very difficult to poison a fowl with daboia-poison without causing primary convulsions, it can with ease be done in the following way :—

Experiment XX.

Five centigrammes (or ·77 grain) of dried daboia-poison were dissolved in one cubic centimetre of water, and heated for a short time to 100° C. (212° F.). The solution was then cooled, and injected subcutaneously into the leg of a fowl.

12.27 P.M. Injection.

12.34 P.M. Seems drowsy ; eyes closed.

12.45 P.M. Breathing rapid.

12.47 P.M. Respiration failing; comb becoming purple.

12.49 P.M. Lying down ; head drooping.

12.50 P.M. Fallen over on its side; respiration fainter.

12.53 P.M. Gasping.

12.56 P.M. Convulsions.

12.58 P.M. Convulsions lessening.

12.59 P.M. Dead.

Here, though the amount of poison injected was more than fifteen times that required to cause almost instant death from convulsions, simple exposure to a heat of 100° C. completely altered the symptoms. They were those of gradual paralysis which caused the respiration to cease, and the convulsions were evidently simply the expression of carbonic acid poisoning; they were secondary, and no longer primary.

In regard to the paralysis subsequently caused by daboia-poison, there are one or two points to be observed. It certainly supervenes earlier than in cobra-poisoning, but it does not extinguish the respiratory function nearly so soon. Paraplegia is occasionally noticed in dogs, especially if the hind-legs have been much convulsed. Care, however, should be taken not to confound it with inability to use the hind-quarters from the pain occasioned by the injection of the poison, which appears to be peculiarly severe. In fact, if the hind-legs be never used for poisoning in dogs, paraplegia will be very rarely indeed described, even in daboia-poisoning.

Again, the paralysis of the tongue and larynx, which

is such a marked symptom of cobra-poisoning, is absent in daboia-poisoning. The tongue, it is true, may be sometimes pendulous during part of the time; but it is usually retracted into the mouth before death, which never happens in cobra-poisoning. Moreover, the larynx is not paralysed, the dog groaning, screaming, and barking, even when his limbs are powerless. It seems as if the poison exerted its influence on the main motor tract, and did not possess the marked affinity for certain centres that cobra-poison has; a circumstance for which the method in which it commences its action, and the time that it takes to extinguish the respiratory function, might have prepared us.

Action of Daboia-Poison on Respiration.

When primary convulsions occur in daboia-poisoning, the natural respiration is very quickly abolished. Chart No. 6, taken from a fowl, gives a typical example of the respiration when the primary convulsions are fatal. It contains nearly all the chest movements from the moment of injection of the poison till death. The first sixteen respirations are normal; the excursus is then slightly increased, and a slight retardation is to be observed; then, without further warning, the most violent convulsions took place, and with them life was extinguished. It affords corroborative evidence of the fact that asphyxia has nothing to do with the causation

No. VI.—TRACING OF RESPIRATORY MOVEMENTS IN FOWL UNDER THE INFLUENCE OF DABOIA POISON.

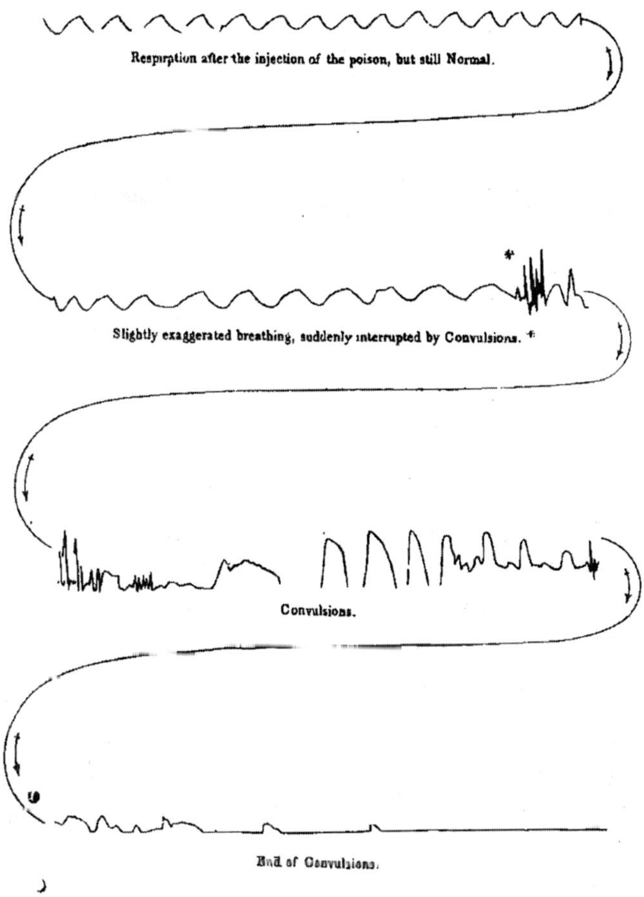

No. VII.—TRACING OF RESPIRATORY MOVEMENT IN A FOWL UNDER THE INFLUENCE OF DABOIA POISON THAT HAD BEEN HEATED TO 100°C.

I

Normal

II

Great acceleration.

III

IV

V

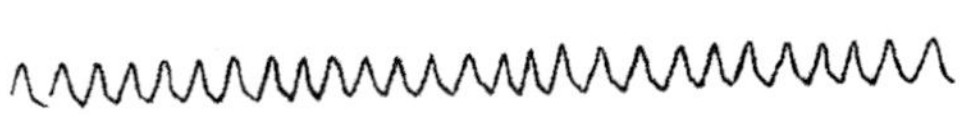

Great acceleration with increased Excursus..

VI

Lessened Excursus.

of the convulsions. Should death not occur at once after the convulsions, respiration is resumed; very slowly at first, then gaining a rapidity far beyond normal, to be again diminished, and finally extinguished. If convulsions do not take place, the rapidity of the respirations becomes extreme.

Chart No. 7 is from a fowl that was poisoned by daboia-poison, which had been heated in solution to a 100° C., and so deprived of its power of causing convulsions. The acceleration of the respiratory movements is most remarkable, as is also the way in which the excursus is exaggerated and maintained; it is only at the very end of life that the respiratory movement is diminished.

Chart No. 8 is from a dog, to which sufficient poison was not given to cause convulsions. The very much greater acceleration of the respiration than can be caused by cobra-poisoning is seen; the respirations in I. and III. being as two to five. But in IV. a singular condition is to be noticed, which is exceedingly common in daboia-poisoning. The respiration has become slower, but the excursus is increased; but the peculiarity is that ordinary respiration is occasionally interrupted—it may be once in six, to once in twenty respirations—by a very prolonged and excessive upheaving of the chest-walls. If the phenomenon be examined, when well marked, it will be found that a deep inspiration is first taken, and when the diaphragm has descended, the muscles of the abdominal wall contract forcibly, the glottis is closed, the legs are drawn up over the abdomen, the perineum is bulged out; then suddenly relaxation occurs, and the ordinary respiratory rhythm is resumed. As the paralysis becomes more marked this gradually fades into a deep inspiration, and this, in its turn, is abolished, the respiration becoming slower, though the excursus is maintained in a remarkable way.

Daboia-poisoning is characterised, then, by the long time it takes to abolish respiration after the body paralysis is complete, and by the very irregular character of the respiratory movements during the progress of the paralysis, and also by the very great acceleration that occurs in the earlier stages and the increased excursus. The two species of poisoning could be distinguished from one another in the vast majority of cases by the character of the respiration alone. It is very unusual for the convulsions of asphyxia to occur in daboia-poisoning if the primary convulsions have been at all marked.

Effect of Daboia-Poison on the Circulation, Temperature, Special Senses, Secretion, and the Blood.

In regard to its influence on the temperature and circulation, it cannot be said that daboia-poisoning differs much from cobra-poisoning. The temperature is

No. VIII.—TRACINGS OF RESPIRATORY MOVEMENTS OF DOG UNDER DABOIA POISONING.

Normal Respiration.

II

Acceleration.

III.

Respiration still quicker

IV

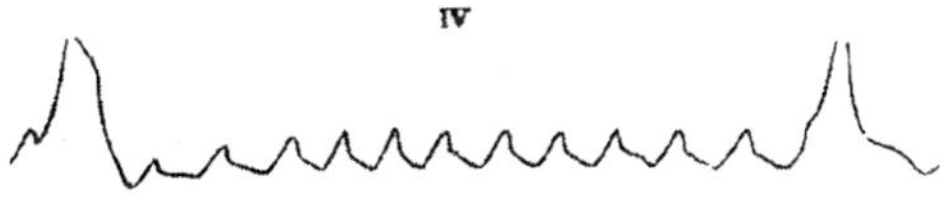

Irregular Respiration.

V

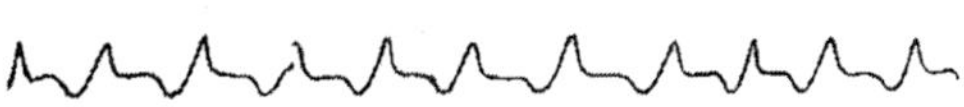

Respiration slowing.

VI

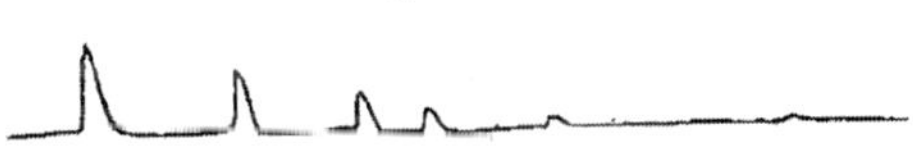

End of Respiratory movements.

but slightly, if at all, raised in ordinary cases of daboia-poisoning, and the circulation can be maintained long after complete paralysis has occurred and the respiration has stopped, if the blood be kept oxygenated by artificial means.

On the pupil it seems as if daboia-poison had some influence. After the primary convulsions have ceased, the pupil is nearly always, if not always, widely dilated. This dilatation is not dependent on asphyxia, as it is often present when the convulsions are absent. The iris becomes merely a narrow ring; but at the later stages the pupil becomes again contracted, often being smaller than natural. If life is prolonged by artificial respiration, the pupil remains somewhat contracted, to dilate again on artificial respiration being discontinued, It would, of course, require direct observation on the human subject to ascertain the effect which daboia-poison exerts on accommodation.

Over secretion daboia-poison also has some power. Mucous discharges occur from mucous tracts with considerable frequency; but it is infinitely less powerful in causing salivation than cobra-poison. If the experiments given at the commencement of this section be looked at, in not one is salivation recorded. If the elaborate series of experiments in Sir J. Fayrer's "Thanatophidia" be examined, it will be seen that in not a single experiment with daboia-poison is the word "salivation" used, whereas it is constantly employed in describing cases of cobra-poisoning. I am, however, satisfied that it does sometimes occur, having seen it once in a very slight degree. But it is so rare that it cannot be considered as anything but very exceptional; and it will not be going too far to say that in dogs it is as rare to see salivation in daboia-poisoning as it is to see it absent in cobra-poisoning.

In daboia-poisoning there is a good deal of evidence to be considered as to the effect of the poison on the blood. It is almost universally found that the blood is incoagulable; the only exceptions being when an animal dies almost instantaneously from the convulsions, and also when it dies after a very long interval from exhaustion. The first condition is often found in fowls, and the second in robust animals which have had only a small quantity of poison administered to them. In the first class of cases it is probable that sufficient time has not elapsed for blood changes to occur; in the second the blood has had time, to a certain extent, to regain its normal character, for in these cases the coagulation is somewhat imperfect. In addition to the loss of coagulability of the blood, even in the lower animals, we have proof that the relation of the blood to the tissues is altered. Even in rapid cases of daboia-poisoning, hæmorrhages from the mucous membranes are exceedingly common. Exudations of blood beneath the conjunctiva and mucous membrane of the mouth are also sometimes seen. So grave are the changes in the blood, that it is not unusual for an animal to die of the consequences of them alone, without a single nerve symptom having occurred. Thus in Experiment III. the animal had no symptom till the respirations began to increase in frequency, nor did the animal show any muscular weakness then; the only evidence that there was of any other abnormal condition being copious discharges of sanious fluid from the mouth and rectum. The sole cause of death was undoubtedly œdema of the pulmonary tissue, and the antecedent condition to this must have been simply the altered condition of the blood. But it is easy to collect plenty of cases of death from blood change in daboia-poison.

Experiment XXI.

A cat had one cubic centimetre of a solution of daboia-poison, containing about five milligrammes (·077 of a grain) of the poison injected into its leg subcutaneously.

3.3 P.M. Injection.

3.16 P.M. Seems in some pain.

3.37 P.M. Respiration somewhat rapid.

7 P.M. Seems pretty well.

6 A.M. Ill; vomiting.

1 P.M. Crouches down, disinclined to be disturbed.

7 P.M. Refuses food.

This animal lived for four days, all the time refusing food, having diarrhœa, and at last died of exhaustion. The blood was found to be feebly coagulated after death.

Experiment XXII.

A solution of about five milligrammes (·077 of a grain) of daboia-poison was injected into a dog.

4 P.M. Injection.

7 P.M. No symptom.

8 A.M. No change.

4 P.M. As no symptom appeared, five milligrammes more daboia-poison were injected.

7 P.M. No change.

9.30 P.M. Affected; respirations 50; pupils widely dilated.

6 A.M. Still seems ill, but can stand.

2 P.M. Depressed and ill.

3 P.M. Passed some albuminous urine.

9 P.M. Not much change; diarrhœa.

6 A.M. Still very ill.

12 P.M. Urine albuminous; seems very ill.

As it was clear that the animal would die a lingering death, as in the last experiment, some more daboia-poison was injected to shorten life.

1.30 P.M. Injection.

3.9 P.M. Passed a sanious motion.

3.17 P.M. Cannot stand.

3.20 P.M. Respiration failing.

3.29 P.M. Dead.

These were two cases of severe blood-poisoning which occurred almost completely without accompanying nerve symptoms, one of which was fatal, and the other undoubtedly would have been had the case been allowed to run its course.

In cobra-poisoning pure and simple albuminuria is unknown; but in every case of daboia-poisoning in which symptoms were present, and in which six hours elapsed before death, I have detected albumen in the urine. It is generally not in very large quantity, but is still unmistakable. Care should be taken not to allow the urine secreted before the commencement of the symptoms to mix with that secreted after.

There is evidence, therefore, that daboia venom is a most severe blood-poison, producing death when not administered in sufficient quantities to cause serious nerve symptoms, and that it is even possible for death to occur quite early from this cause alone, nerve symptoms not having supervened.

The following case, related by Dr. F. M. Mackenzie, shows the insidious nature of blood-poisoning induced by the venom of vipers. The suake was probably the *Echis carinata,* a congener of the daboia:—

A Mahomedan, aged forty, was bitten by a snake about a foot long, with rough scales, called by the natives "corella," on one of his fingers. The region of the bite was soon after incised, but the hand and arm became much swollen. He vomited, and the same day passed blood with his urine and fæces, and his vomit contained blood. The third day the temperature was

101° F. The fifth day the temperature was 99°·4 F., and the symptoms remained unabated. He suffered from hiccough, and the hæmorrhage was unchecked. He gradually grew weaker from the loss of blood, and consequently died of exhaustion on the ninth day.

It would be difficult to find a greater contrast to this case of viper-poisoning than that of Dr. Richards's instance of cobra-poisoning, where the man, after suffering from severe nerve symptoms, was on the second day quite well.

There are in this case two points of interest. The first is that the temperature was but very slightly raised during the progress of the disease; and the other, that the symptoms, though they required so long a time to prove fatal, yet commenced almost directly after the infliction of the bite. It should be stated, also, that even after the symptoms of hæmorrhage have showed themselves a complete recovery is possible. We may conclude, then, that in this form of poisoning, when the nerve effects have quite passed away, there remains a period of blood-poisoning as fatal to life as the nerve symptoms themselves.

In daboia-poisoning general muscular weakness is much more marked than in cobra-poisoning. The heart's action especially gives evidence of its weakened muscular condition, which appears often to be the immediate cause of death.

Summary of the Difference of the Effects of Daboia and Cobra Poison.

From the above examination of the symptoms produced by the two poisons, the following summary of the differences in their effects may be made.

Cobra-poison, when introduced slowly into the circulation, produces gradual general paralysis, but at the same time shows a preference for certain nerve centres, —paralysis of the tongue, lips, and larynx, being very marked symptoms,—and respiration is very quickly extinguished after the paralysis shows itself. Death is often attended by convulsions, which are clearly due to carbonic-acid poisoning.

Introduced with a fair amount of rapidity, these symptoms are rapidly developed, the paralysis being preceded by gentle stimulation, which causes slight muscular twitchings.

Injected in a large quantity into the circulation, the stimulation is so violent as to cause general convulsions, of which, however, the respiratory muscles have the chief share, and which are immediately followed by paralysis and death.

Daboia-poison, though not injected directly into the circulation, causes directly the most violent convulsions, which are in no way necessarily followed by immediate paralysis and death, but may be for the time completely recovered from. They do not depend on carbonic-acid poisoning. The paralysis that succeeds is general, and lasts a very considerable time before respiration is extinguished. There is no evidence of the tongue, lips and larynx being especially paralysed; they probably only suffer in the same degree as the other parts.

Cobra-poison very quickly destroys the respiratory function: after slight acceleration the respiration becomes slower and the excursus is lessened.

Daboia-poison at first quickens the respiration very much more than cobra-poison does, and the lessening of the excursus and the slowing of the breathing do not occur so soon. The respiration generally in daboia-poisoning has a peculiarly irregular character. This function certainly exists longer under the influence of daboia-poison than under that of cobra-poison.

The effect of cobra-poison on the pupil is so slight as to be a matter of doubt; daboia-poison nearly always causes wide dilatation in the earlier stages of the poisoning.

Salivation is a constant symptom of cobra-poisoning; it is exceedingly rare in daboia-poisoning.

The effect of cobra-poison on the blood is not very great, sanious discharges are rare, albuminuria has not been seen, and recovery is striking and complete.

In daboia-poisoning, on the other hand, sanious discharges are the rule, albuminuria is usual should the victim live any time, and after the nerve symptoms have passed away the subject has to go through a period of blood-poisoning little, if at all, less dangerous than the primary symptoms. We have, in addition, the greater local mischief caused by daboia-poison, and the greater power it has of destroying the coagulability of the blood.

The physiological properties of daboia-poison undergo great change by its being heated to 100° C. in solution, losing the power of producing primary convulsions, whereas cobra-poison remains unaltered.

Daboia-poison kills birds at once in convulsions, whereas with cobra-poison—unless the poison has been directly injected into the circulation—death occurs only after paralysis.

Lastly, amphibia recover from an amount of daboia-poison that would be necessarily fatal in the case of cobra-poison.

CHAPTER III.

THE PHYSIOLOGICAL EFFECTS PRODUCED BY THE POISONS OF THE BUNGARUS FASCIATUS AND THE BUNGARUS CŒRULEUS.

THE Bungarus fasciatus is a snake that has a very wide distribution in India. It is common in Bengal, extends down the Coromandel coast and into Burmah, where it is said to entirely replace its congener, the Bungarus cœruleus. It is also common in Java, the Malayan Peninsula, Penang, Tenasserim, and China. It is of shy, retiring habits, and is not easily irritated. The natives of India are of opinion that it never hisses, but I have several times heard it do so, but very gently. It is not possible to determine what share it contributes to the general mortality from snake-bite. It belongs, of course, to the colubrine division of snakes, and is easily recognised by the alternate bands of black and yellow that surround its body. The effects of its poison are demonstrated by the following experiments.

Experiment I.

A medium-sized pariah dog had a pulse of 72 beats and 32 respirations per minute.

2.50 P.M. Bitten by a Bungarus fasciatus.

3.1 P.M. Respirations 27.

3.37 P.M. Retching.

3.47 P.M. Vomiting.

3.48 P.M. Respirations 36.

4.1 P.M. Respirations 28.

4.5 P.M. Staggering.

4.16 P.M. Hardly able to stand.

4.17 P.M. Respirations 26.

4.20 P.M. Pupils contracted.

4.21 P.M. Respirations 24.

4.33 P.M. Lying at full length, apparently unconscious. Can be, however, roused, when it tries to rise, but is unable.

4.35 P.M. Pulse 85; fore and hind limbs equally paralysed.

4.39 P.M. Respirations 22.

4.50 P.M. Discharge from nostrils. The dog was now bitten by another Bungarus fasciatus.

4.54 P.M. Respirations 20.

5.2 P.M. Tongue hanging out of the mouth.

5.7 P.M. Respirations 16.

5.25 P.M. Pulse 72.

5.50 P.M. Slight twitchings of the muscles of the extremities.

5.59 P.M. Respirations 13.

6 P.M. Convulsions.

6.5 P.M. Salivation.

6.23 P.M. Convulsions.

6.24 P.M. Respiratory movement ceased.

6.26 P.M. Dead.

Experiment II.

A cat was bitten on the leg by a Bungarus fasciatus.

1.7 P.M. Bitten.

2 P.M. The leg which was bitten is swollen.

6.30 P.M. Affected; sluggish; staggers when roused.

7.8 P.M. Becoming paralysed.

7.15 P.M. Respiration failing.

7.37 P.M. Lying down; respiration almost ceased; a small quantity of clear fluid running from the mouth; commencing convulsions.

7.43 P.M. Convulsions stronger.

7.46 P.M. All movement ceased; pupils dilated.

7.47½ P.M. Heart stopped. Dead.

Experiment III.

A strong healthy pariah dog was bitten in the centre of the back by a Bungarus fasciatus.

1.20 P.M. Bitten.

1.56 P.M. Vomited.

1.58 P.M. Looks somewhat depressed; site of bite much swollen.

2.4 P.M. Vomited some frothy mucus.

2.39 P.M. Slightly unsteady in gait.

2.46 P.M. Fell over.

2.57 P.M. Pupils dilated; salivation; tongue hanging out of mouth; respiration stopped.

2.59 P.M. Dead.

Rigor mortis was well marked; blood coagulated; kidneys and lungs very much congested.

Experiment IV.

A cat was bitten by a Bungarus fasciatus.

2.45 P.M. Bitten.

7 A.M. Somewhat depressed; has vomited.

11.30 A.M. Affected; can hardly stand.

12.10 P.M. Vomiting.

12.37 P.M. Copious salivation.

12.47 P.M. Vomiting frothy mucus.

3.38 P.M. Very weak.

4.12 P.M. Passed some albuminous urine.

7.39 P.M. Cannot stand; respirations 80, but the movement is very slight.

9.7 P.M. Dead.

There was coagulation of the blood after death.

Experiment V.

A small pariah dog was bitten by a Bungarus fasciatus.

12.33 P.M. Bitten.

12.40 P.M. Bitten spot swollen.

1.17 P.M. Affected ; staggering.

1.35 P.M. Unable to stand.

1.36 P.M. Salivated.

1.38 P.M. Twitchings of muscles of limbs.

1.39 P.M. Occasional spasm of diaphragm.

1.40 P.M. Pupils normal.

1.41 P.M. Tongue protruded.

1.43 P.M. Respirations reduced to an occasional inspiratory spasm.

1.56 P.M. Dead.

Experiment VI.

A pariah dog was bitten by a Bungarus fasciatus. The snake had been some time in captivity.

Noon. Bitten.

1st Day—

12.19 P.M. Had some general irregular muscular contractions, after which it seemed somewhat paralysed.

12.35 P.M. Seems quite well again.

2nd Day. Quite well.

3rd Day. No symptom.

4th Day. No change.

5th Day. Somewhat depressed; refused food.

6th Day. Lying down ; very weak ; temperature 103°·2 F.; respiratory movement somewhat lessened ; urine (the first passed since the 2nd day) slightly albuminous, contains casts of renal tubes; pupils normal.

7th Day. No change in the symptoms, but is much weaker.

8th Day. Died in the night.

Rigor mortis fairly marked; lungs œdematous; blood feebly coagulated; kidneys congested; bladder empty.

Experiment VII.

A large healthy pariah dog was bitten by a Bungarus fasciatus.

1st Day—

12.38 P.M. Bitten.

12.44 P.M. Site of bite swollen.

12.46 P.M. Respirations 24.

12.47 P.M. Pulse 84.

12.50 P.M. Temperature in rectum 102°·7 F.

7 P.M. No symptom.

2nd Day. No change.

3rd Day. Quite well.

4th Day. Without any symptom.

5th Day—

7 A.M. No change.

7 P.M. Looks depressed; no special symptom.

6th Day—

7 A.M. Appears ill.

4 P.M. Pulse 130. Respirations 20. Temperature in rectum 102°·2 F.

7 P.M. Ate sparingly of food.

10.12 P.M. Pulse 132. Respirations 30. Has vomited.

7th Day—

7 A.M. Is very weak, but no special symptom; can walk, but soon lies down.

7 P.M. Ate a little meat, which he retained.

8th Day—

8.15 A.M. Passed about six ounces of urine; the first for four days.

8.36 A.M. Respirations 20.

8.37 A.M. Pulse 134.

8.45 A.M. Temperature in rectum 102°·4 F.

5.5 P.M. Appears ill, and is very weak.

5.6 P.M. Respirations 40. Pupils dilated.

5.7 P.M. Pulse 160.

5.10 P.M. Temperature in rectum 103°·9 F.

7 P.M. Very weak. Ate sparingly of food.

11.25 P.M. Slightly stertorous breathing.

9th Day—

2.3 A.M. Vomiting.

7 A.M. Extremely weak; unable to stand.

2.55 P.M. Respirations 24.

2.56 P.M. Pulse 108.

2.59 P.M. Temperature 101°·2 F.

3 P.M. Pupils normal. Tongue slightly pendulous. There is a purulent discharge from the eyes and nose.

3.47 P.M. Passed four ounces of urine; it is albuminous, and contains fibrinous casts of the renal tubes.

3.56 P.M. Died after a few jactitations of the limbs. The blood coagulated soon after death.

Experiment VIII.

A pariah dog was bitten by a Bungarus fasciatus.

1st Day—

11.45 A.M. Bitten.

7 P.M. No change.

2nd Day—

Site of bite swollen, but no constitutional symptom.

3rd Day—

7 A.M. Appears weak. Respirations 56.

11.17 A.M. Very depressed.

12.30 P.M. Passed some albuminous urine.

2.25 P.M. Occasional spasm of diaphragm.

3 P.M. Is weak, but can stand.

5.21 P.M. Pulse 150. Respirations 24.

5.29 P.M. Dead.

Blood feebly coagulated. Slight œdema of lungs.

Experiment IX.

A fowl was bitten on the leg by a Bungarus fasciatus; Its respirations, immediately before it was bitten, were 36 per minute.

1.18 P.M. Bitten.

1.19 P.M. Bitten leg drawn up.

1.24 P.M. Respirations 40.

1.25 P.M. Head drooping till the beak touches the ground.

1.27 P.M. Cannot stand.

1.28 P.M. Pupils normal Respirations 28.

1.31 P.M. Respirations 10 per minute; slight muscular twitchings.

1.32 P.M. Convulsions.

1.33 P.M. Dead.

The blood coagulated firmly.

It will be seen at a glance that these experiments can be divided into two distinct classes, having scarcely any feature in common. The first five experiments, and the ninth, belong to one class; and the sixth, seventh, and eighth, to the other. Experiment V. may be taken as a typical example of the first class. It will be seen that in the beginning there is a manifestation of local inflammation at the site of the bite, and that there is a considerable pause before any constitutional signs are manifested. Then follow salivation, commencing paralysis, twitchings of the muscles of the extremities, paralysis of the tongue, cessation of the respiration, and death. In Experiment I. the same course of symptoms occurs. There is retching, vomiting, gradually advancing general paralysis, muscular twitchings, paralysis of the tongue, salivation, convulsions and death. In all these, the exact course of symptoms described in cobra-poisoning is to be observed, and it would not be possible, from watching a case of this kind to decide whether it was an instance of cobra-poisoning, or of poisoning by the Bungarus fasciatus, that was under observation. The only difference that can be pointed out is in the time that elapses before death occurs. Thus, in the two cases given of death from the bite of the cobra, seventy-three minutes and twenty-two minutes elapsed respectively before death; whereas, the shortest time in the case of the Bungarus fasciatus was eighty-three minutes before a small dog succumbed, and a large dog lived ninety-nine minutes; and a medium-sized dog survived no less than three hours and thirty-six minutes, and all the symptoms were much more gradual in their accession, and lasted a longer time. In birds, too, the symptoms are exactly those of cobra-poisoning, only they are also more prolonged.

But if the Experiments VI., VII., and VIII. are examined, an entirely different set of phenomena is to be observed. Thus, if Experiment VII. is taken, we find that for five complete days after being bitten, the animal remained in perfect health. At the end of this period the dog appeared indisposed, and from this time a disease commenced, having marked definite features, which proved fatal on the ninth day. The most singular feature in this condition is the long interval that occurs between the infliction of the bite and the occurrence of any symptom. It appears to vary from two to six days. Nothing like this is known in cobra-poisoning, where, if the victim does not succumb soon, a complete recovery is to be anticipated; or from daboia-poisoning, where the hæmorrhages that destroy life begin in a few hours, though they may last for a lengthened period before the sufferer's life is extinguished. This interval, in this chronic form of poisoning by the Bungarus fasciatus, calls to mind strongly that similar period which occurs between exposure to the poison and the development of most infectious diseases. It is, in fact, a period of *incubation*, and we thus see snake-poison allying itself in its effects to those subtle contagia so remarkable for their profound constitutional results. The disease, in this chronic form of poisoning by the Bungarus fasciatus, once developed, pursues its course, no case under my observation having recovered after the symptoms had once begun.

But even when the constitutional effects of the poison of the Bungarus fasciatus do manifest themselves after this period of incubation, they no longer resemble, in any particular, the acute form of poisoning, either of the Bungarus fasciatus or the cobra; but they have a character and course of their own. The first thing noticed is loss of appetite, with great depression, and diminution of urinary secretion. Then there is slight failure of the respiratory function, irregular but considerable elevations of temperature, and great muscular weakness. Purulent discharges take place from the eyes, nose, and rectum, but there is no tendency to hæmorrhage. There is albumen in the urine, but no blood or hæmal colouring-matter. There is no special paralysis of the tongue and larynx. At last death ends the exhausted condition to which the victim has been reduced. The symptoms, it will be seen, are equally distinct, on the one hand, from those of the acute form, or from cobra-poisoning; and on the other, from daboia or viper-poisoning. The contrast between this poison and that of the cobra is most striking. In cobra-poisoning, the most prolonged fatal case on record took forty-nine hours and nine minutes, and it was shown in treating of that poison that even very severe symptoms might be completely recovered from. But in the case of poisoning by the Bungarus fasciatus, we cannot for certain say till after five days have elapsed whether we may have to deal with a fatal disease or not.

LOCAL EFFECTS OF THE BITE OF THE BUNGARUS FASCIATUS.

There is, after the bite of this snake, the same local pain produced as in the case of the other snakes described. The condition of the parts, also, is one of inflammation, but the discolouration is much less than that found in cobra-bite; but there is usually a large quantity of pale pinkish serum effused in the areolar tissue, so that considerable local swelling is common. In all the cases I have examined, there has been much greater local change than could possibly be accounted for by the mechanical injury. In those chronic cases terminating fatally after incubation, the site of the wound generally suppurates during the progress of the disease, but this sometimes occurs when no fatal condition is developed, though to a much smaller extent. In one fatal case, also, the only local manifestation was an indurated state of the part, which was found to be highly infiltrated, and somewhat hyperæmic in the centre.

Effect of the Poison of the Bungarus Fasciatus on the Nervous System.

In the acute form of poisoning by this snake, the symptoms show clearly that the chief, if not the sole, cause of death is the effect of the poison on the nervous system. The earliest sign is often an unsteadiness of gait, affecting all the limbs equally, attended by slight clonic contractions of the muscles, rapidly succeeded by paralysis, the respiration at the same time beginning to fail. The pupils remain normal, but the paralysis of the lips, tongue, larynx and pharynx is as strongly marked as in cobra-poisoning. Vomiting also occurs early. There is, in fact, a complete parallelism in the effect of the poison of the cobra and that of the Bungarus fasciatus in the acute form.

In the chronic cases of poisoning by this snake, it is difficult to judge how far the nervous system is involved in the complicated state of disease that has been induced. In Experiment VII., on the first day on which any change was noticed, being the sixth day from the receipt of the bite, there was vomiting, but it could hardly have been the direct effect of the presence of the poison after this interval; it was probably a result of the general disease that was in course of development. The other prominent symptom was the great weakness manifested; the animal became exceedingly feeble, but there did not seem to be any sign of paralysis; the symptom seemed to be due entirely to general muscular debility, caused by the disease. In the same experiment, on the eighth day, there was seen slight pendulousness of the tongue; but this special sign, so marked in the acute cases, was absent in the other instances of chronic poisoning by this snake.

In birds, the nervous symptoms present are exactly those of cobra-poisoning. There is drowsiness, with inability to keep the eyes open, general paralysis rapidly advancing, asphyxia, and death.

Effect of the Poison of the Bungarus Fasciatus on Respiration.

As a rule, the extinction of respiration by this poison is a very slow and gradual process. The stethometric chart No. IX., depicts the chief changes that occur in the usual course. They were taken from a fowl which succumbed quickly to the effects. It will be seen that at first there was slight quickening and increased excursus, but that retardation and lessened movement followed very soon, and that before convulsions occurred the respiratory function was completely abolished. The primary stimulation, however, does not appear to be quite as great as in cobra-poisoning, and if Experiment I. be examined, it will be seen that after the respirations had been reduced from 36 to 20 by the poison, an additional quantity of venom had no power to increase the number of respirations. The fact that after retardation of the respiration has once occurred no acceleration can be caused by more poison being given, shows how dead to stimuli the respiratory centre rapidly becomes under the influence of colubrine venom. In the nature of the respiration during this form of poisoning, little difference can be detected between it and that seen under cobra-poisoning. The main distinction between the two is the greater rapidity with which cobra-poison acts; however, Experiment V., where the dog died in eighty-three minutes, seemed, in all essential particulars, like a case of ordinary cobra-poisoning.

No. IX TRACINGS OF THE RESPIRATORY MOVEMENTS OF A FOWL UNDER THE INFLUENCE OF THE POISON OF THE BUNGARUS FASCIATUS.

I.

Normal respiration.

II.

Respiration slightly quickened with increased excursus.

III.

Excursus greatly lessened.

IV.

Commencing slowing.

V.

Both slowing and lessening excursus.

VI.

Movement very slight

VII.

Respiratory movement abolished and commencing convulsions.

Effect of the Poison of the Bungarus Fasciatus on the Temperature, Secretion, and the Blood.

It will be seen that no change in the temperature was noticed during the acute form of poisoning by the Bungarus fasciatus, any more than is to be seen in cobra-poisoning. In the chronic form, however, there is evidence of considerable influence on the heat of the body. In Experiment VII., during the period of incubation no change was experienced; but with the accession of the symptoms the temperature rose, so that on the eighth day the thermometer marked 103°·9 F., but before death the temperature again fell. In Experiment VI., again, on the sixth day the thermometer was at 103°·2 F. It is clear, therefore, that a febrile movement of considerable intensity occurs during the period of chronic poisoning, but that the interval of incubation is quite free from it.

In acute cases, in its influence on secretion the poison of the Bungarus fasciatus does not differ from cobra-poison. Profuse salivation is common, and vomiting of mucus is often seen; but the urine seems unaffected. In chronic poisoning after incubation, salivation has not been observed, but there is great diminution of urine. The urine, when the diseased condition is established, is scanty, high-coloured, it contains no blood structure, but has in it a considerable quantity of albumen. It will also be found to contain large numbers of casts of the renal tubes. These casts have a very pronounced outline, and appear to be somewhat fibrinous at their edges. In one case, after death distinct fibrinous concretions were found in the pelves of the kidneys.

In addition to this, the whole of the mucous tracts of the body appear to be affected with a tendency to secrete a thin muco-pus. The discharge runs from the eyes, nose, rectum, and vagina; but it differs completely from the sanious discharges seen during viper-poisoning.

The blood in animals after death from the poison of the Bungarus fasciatus is found to coagulate, but in very chronic cases the coagulum formed is of a loose and imperfect character.

Physiological Effects of the Poison of the Bungarus Cœruleus.

The following experiments show the symptoms that are produced by the poison of the Bungarus cœruleus. This snake has a wide distribution over the plains of India, and, from its frequenting inhabited places, probably contributes very largely indeed to the mortality from snake-bite in India.

Experiment X.

A small pariah dog was bitten by a Bungarus cœruleus.

3.15 P.M. Bitten.

3.25 P.M. Affected ; vomiting.

3.27 P.M. Chewing movement of the jaw and lips.

3.29 P.M. Salivation.

3.30 P.M. Tongue hanging out of the mouth ; pupils somewhat contracted ; becoming paralysed.

3.31 P.M. Convulsions.

3.33 P.M. All movement ceased.

3.35 P.M. Pupils dilated.

3.35½ P.M. Heart stopped. Dead.

There was no albumen in the urine.

Experiment XI.

A small quantity of fresh poison from the Bungarus cœruleus was injected subcutaneously into a dog.

1.25 P.M. Injection.

1.40 P.M. Temperature in rectum 102°·6 F.

1.42 P.M. Vomited.

1.45 P.M. Salivation.

1.46 P.M. Pupils somewhat dilated, but answer to light.

1.48 P.M. Vomited mucus.

1.49 P.M. Urinated—urine normal; pupils dilated; staggering; all the legs equally affected; frothy salivation.

1.50 P.M. Unable to stand ; muscular twitchings.

1.54 P.M. Temperature in rectum 102°·6 F.

1.55 P.M. Convulsions.

1.56 P.M. Tongue hanging out of the mouth.

1.59 P.M. Heart only acting.

2 P.M. Dead.

The blood coagulated after death.

Experiment XII.

A fowl was bitten by a Bungarus cœruleus.

2.3 P.M. Bitten.

2.10 P.M. Wings drooping.

2.11 P.M. Eyes closed.

2.12 P.M. Gasping respiration.

2.13 P.M. Cannot stand; head drooping.

2.14 P.M. Beak resting on the ground.

2.16 P.M. Convulsions.

2.20 P.M. Dead.

In all these experiments there is not one point of difference to be detected between the symptoms and those present during cobra-poisoning. In regular order we have vomiting, salivation, twitching of the muscles of the extremities, special glosso-laryngeal paralysis, gradually advancing general paralysis, the convulsions of asphyxia, and death. There is absence of albuminuria and of local hæmorrhage. The poison appears to be identical in its effects with cobra-poison, and even in virulence it does not suffer in contrast with it, for the dog in Experiment X. died in twenty minutes and a half. But though its effects are also exactly those of its congener the Bungarus fasciatus, in the acute form of poisoning by that snake, I have not been able to produce the chronic form of poisoning. It is, of course, probable that the chronic form may occur with this snake also, but the evidence of such a condition occurring is at present negative. But the snakes used in these experiments were very large and vigorous, and would naturally cause the poisoning to be acute.

In regard to the local inflammation produced by the poison of the Bungarus cœruleus, it is, like the Bungarus fasciatus, very much less than that caused by cobra-poison, and has seemed in some instances even less than that of its congener. There is, however, always to be seen some amount of pale serum which is quite enough to satisfy the practised eye that there is something present beyond the effect of mere mechanical injury.

It may be mentioned here that the Echis carinata, or the smaller Indian viper, has, from the cases reported in which its poison proved fatal, precisely the same symptoms as the daboia. There can be little doubt that it contributes very largely to the mortality from snake-bite, especially in Northern and Western India.

CHAPTER IV.

THE RELATIVE POWER AND PROPERTIES OF THE POISONS OF INDIAN AND OTHER VENOMOUS SNAKES.

In the preceding chapters attention has been directed solely to the leading species of Indian venomous snakes, and the differences that exist between the poisons of the colubrine and viperine tribes. Before proceeding to consider the effects of any other snakes, it will be well to sum up the points of which these differences consist.

In viper-poisoning, as seen in the case of the daboia, there is first, if a fair quantity of poison be introduced, intense and sudden general primary convulsions, which may be at once fatal or may rapidly be succeeded by general paralysis and death, or they may be recovered from to a certain extent, paralysis and death following later. The paralysis, which may occur without convulsions, is general, and does not affect any special nerve centres, and is attended also with great muscular weakness. The breathing is at one period exceedingly accelerated, and the pupil is greatly dilated. Even if paralysis should not supervene, the victim may yet die after a prolonged interval, of the effects of profuse sanguineous discharges, which, however, begin soon after the injection of the poison, there being no period of incubation.

In colubrine-poisoning, as seen with the cobra, there are no primary convulsions, with the exception of those cases in which there is injection of a large quantity of poison directly into the circulation. The increase in the rapidity of the respiration is slight, and is quickly followed by retardation. Paralysis rapidly succeeds, which is peculiarly distinguished by special paralysis of the lips, tongue, larynx and pharynx. Salivation is an almost constant symptom. Death may be preceded by the secondary convulsions of asphyxia. Should death not occur soon, the symptoms pass off, and speedy convalescence is established. In the case of the poison of the Bungarus fasciatus, a special form of chronic poisoning may occur. It differs from the chronic poisoning of the daboia by coming on only after a long incubation which is passed without any symptom, and which may be prolonged to as long as five or six days. The main features of this condition are excessive muscular weakness, severe fever, albuminuria, purulent discharges from mucous surfaces, and death from exhaustion. There is no special tendency to hæmorrhages.

It is, therefore, equally distinct from the acute form of colubrine-poisoning, and from the fatal chronic form due to viperine-poisoning.

It will be of great utility here to consider what light can be thrown on the subject of the differences of snake-poisons by the evidence that is obtainable as to the actions of the poisons of snakes belonging to the fauna of other countries.

Concerning Australian snake-poisoning, the best reported case appears in the Appendix to the Report on "Indian and Australian Snake-Poisoning," by Drs. Ewart, Richards and Mackenzie. The snake by which the poison was injected was either the Pseudechis porphyriacus or the Hoplocephalus curtus; both of them are colubrine snakes.

The following is the case :—

A dog weighing 26 lbs. was bitten by a snake at 11.22 A.M.

11.39 A.M. Vomited twice.

11.43 A.M. Is restless, vomited.

11.52 A.M. Vomited, and is purged.

NOON. Vomited bloody mucus.

12.30 P.M. Vomited white frothy viscid mucus.

1 P.M. Lying down very drowsy, breathing quietly, salivation.

1.21 P.M. Tongue partially paralysed.

1·35 P.M. Is slightly convulsed, but is sensible.

1.48 P.M. Eye still sensitive.

1.53 P.M. Heart's action irregular; pupils widely dilated.

1.56 P.M. Eye no longer sensitive.

1.58 P.M. Commenced artificial respiration; eyes at once became sensitive, and the heart's action, which was before weak and slow, became strong and rapid—the heart was beating nearly 200, but on stopping artificial respiration it fell to 80, and gradually failed.

2.11 P.M. Dead.

Here there was gradual general paralysis, with special paralysis of the tongue, vomiting, salivation, and the convulsions of asphyxia and death. The mucus vomited was at one period stained with blood, but this ceased. In fact, in all essential particulars it is a well-marked case of colubrine-poisoning. There is not a sufficiently well-recorded case of snake-poisoning by a Hoplocephalus or Pseudechis in the human subject to quote here; but it may be said, from the symptoms of those cases that have been published, that they resemble in their course the ordinary features of colubrine-poisoning, as seen with the cobra, but with a few minor differences. There is a much greater tendency to vomiting, which is very often stained with blood, as if this was a special effect of the poison. Dilatation of the pupil is very generally mentioned, often, also, swelling of the parotid gland, but this occurs also in cobra-poisoning. From certain remarks made about the vision of the victims, I should not be surprised to find that paralysis of accommodation occurs. In regard to the relative power of the cobra and the Australian colubrine snakes, five cases of cobra-bite in dogs, taken indiscriminately, gave an average time before death of 34·4 minutes; whereas the Australian Hoplocephalus curtus took, in five cases selected on account of their rapidity, an average time of 84 minutes, or about two and a half times as long, and the average time required to destroy human life seems about eighteen hours by the Hoplocephalus. Chronic constitutional poisoning does not seem to occur with this snake, as in no case did death in the human subject occur after forty-eight hours; in one case, in a dog that was hypodermically injected, death took place in sixty-six hours, and this seems the extreme limit, forty-nine hours being the longest period of all the cases of cobra-bite given in Sir Joseph Fayrer's "Thanatophidia."

The literature of American snake-poisoning is also somewhat meagre, but the most valuable information on the subject is undoubtedly contained in Dr. Weir Mitchell's "Researches upon the Venom of the Rattlesnake."

The Crotalus, or American rattle-snake, of which there are many species, is, of course, a viper distinguished both by the peculiarity of its tail, constituting the so-called rattle, and by a depression on the lateral aspect of the head, from which it has sometimes been termed a "pit-viper."

The following case from Dr. Weir Mitchell's work describes the symptoms of poisoning by the Crotalus in the dog. A dog weighing thirty-one pounds, was bitten by a Crotalus. After the bite there was considerable twitching of the muscles around, and great local swelling. The pulse at the fifth minute after the bite was 140, and the respirations 35. At the fifteenth minute he appeared weak, the pulse was 160, and the respirations 40. At the twentieth minute there was some tenesmus, and a loose grey discharge from the rectum. At the twenty-fifth minute the pupil was normal. At the forty-fifth minute, pulse 160, respirations 45, and laborious. Fifty-fifth minute, loss of power in the hind-legs. Eightieth minute, respiration very quick and laboured; and at the third hour the dog was found dead.

The next instance is also from Dr. Weir Mitchell's book. A rabbit was bitten by a snake which, apparently, had nearly been exhausted of its poison. Very soon after, the animal showed signs of weakness, and its respiration became rapid. It then improved somewhat, but the next day it passed a large quantity of blood mixed with fæces, and its urine was very albuminous. These symptoms increased in severity, and the animal died on the third day.

In another case, in which a dog was bitten twice, the first time without effect, five minutes after the infliction of the second bite by a Crotalus, the dog fell on its side and vomited, the vomiting being instantaneously followed by general convulsions, in which the limbs were extended and the head thrown back. The breathing was laborious and often interrupted, the pupils were contracted. The pulse became less frequent and very feeble. The animal died in twenty-four minutes.

In the case of a pigeon, three minutes after the bite it fell down and immediately began breathing convulsively, now and then gasping, and making efforts to rise. At the end of the seventh minute the laboured breathing ceased, and the bird died at once.

In these instances we have in mammals general primary convulsions occurring five minutes after the infliction of the bite, very rapid breathing, followed by general paralysis and death. In one of the cases, also, there was chronic constitutional poisoning commencing directly after the bite, but not proving fatal till the third day. There was, in this case, albuminuria, and passing of blood from the rectum. In no case is salivation or paralysis of the tongue mentioned.

In birds the convulsions seem to be entirely replaced by excessive disorder of the respiratory fuuction. There is gasping, with irregular movements of the chest-walls, and general paralysis supervenes. There seems, also, great muscular weakness. The blood is nearly always found fluid, and even extravasations of blood in the viscera have been found after death.

In its main features, therefore, the Crotalus resembles

the Indian viper in its effects, the chief difference being that the primary convulsions are very much less frequently seen—birds seeming to have in place of them special respiratory irregularities. In regard to its power of destruction, contrasted with that of other snakes, there is some evidence to be considered. In Dr. Weir Mitchell's work four cases of fatal Crotalus poisoning in dogs gave an average of two hours and twenty-six minutes before death, but no fewer than five dogs recovered completely after being bitten. With the Indian cobra and the Australian Hoplocephalus the average length of the period of fatal poisoning was 34·4 minutes and one hour and twenty-four minutes respectively. It is, therefore, much less dangerous than either of these poisons.

As to the probable duration of human life after the bite of a cobra, it is difficult to obtain trustworthy evidence, as the species of snake from which death resulted is, in India, very rarely identified; and it is for this reason, also, that it is impossible to assign to each species its exact share in the general mortality. However, disregarding the species of snake, there is sufficient evidence in Sir Joseph Fayrer's "Thanatophidia" to give a close approximation to the probable duration of life in Indian snake-poisoning. In that work sixty-five cases are given in which the time that elapsed between the infliction of the bite and death is stated. The average length of time of the whole sixty-five cases, is 15·17 hours; but the average is raised by the exceptionally long duration of a few cases of viperine poisoning, so that a better estimate of the probable duration of time will be obtained by dividing the period after the bite into spaces of one hour each, and determining what percentage of deaths occurs in each :—

	Percentage of Deaths.
One hour and under	10·76
Between one and two hours ...	12·3
Between two and three hours ...	13·84
Between three and four hours ...	7·61
Between four and five hours ...	1·54
Between five and six hours	1·54
Between six and seven hours ...	3·07
Between seven and eight hours ...	4·61
Between eight and nine hours ...	3·07
Between nine and ten hours ...	7·69
Between ten and twelve hours ...	4·61
Between twelve and twenty-four hours	9·36
Over twenty-four hours	20·00

From this table it will be seen that the most fatal period is between two and three hours, and that more than twenty-five per cent. of the total deaths take place between one and three hours after the infliction of the bite. But, if those who die after twenty-four hours be eliminated as having occurred, as is probable, from viper-poisoning, it would raise the average of those who die from colubrine-poisoning between two and three hours after the infliction of the bite, to thirty-two per cent.

It may be mentioned here, as bearing on the causes of the differences of the poisons of the two tribes of venomous snakes, that on the duct leading from the poison-gland of the daboia, midway between the gland and its termination at the fang, there is a second gland, completely surrounding the duct, into which it empties. This accessory gland is globular, and is exceedingly vascular. No trace of this structure can be found in the cobra.

The exact significance of the differences between the poisons of the viperine and colubrine snakes must rest at present in obscurity. But it may be well to point out some of the conditions in which the two groups differ, and the possible uses of the poison apparatus. On consideration, it will probably be admitted that as a means of defence the poison would not be of any real assistance. It is true that many animals—such as the monkey—have the greatest dread of snakes; but the monkey could have no possible motive in molesting a cobra, or a cobra in injuring a monkey. This dread, therefore, can hardly be of service to the reptiles. But one of the Indian snakes' chief enemies, the mongoose, has no fear whatever of the poison, as anyone will confess who has seen with what complete ease he seizes the snake and crushes out first one and then the other of the poison fangs with his long incisors, and then devours the cobra—thus rendered helpless—at his leisure. That the mongoose is perfectly aware of the existence of the poison-fang there can be no doubt, for he only seizes the cobra by the fang; and should he miss his aim, he retires at once out of reach, to make a fresh attack. But the presence of the poison certainly does not deter him in the slightest degree from engaging in the struggle, and so does not in the least protect the cobra from him. The enemy also of one kind of snake is the enemy of the race, so that one kind of poison would be of equal assistance as a means of defence to all species. As a protection from enemies, therefore, a case can scarcely be made out in favour of the poison. But as an aid in procuring food, we can see at once that it would avail much. The cobra, living in holes in the jungle and around villages, haunts the water. Deprived of water, it dies very soon. It is a well-known frequenter of the village tank, and visits the neighbouring jheels or ponds, and it is in these localities that it finds its favourite food—the frogs. Now, few animals have such a wonderful tenacity of life as the frog; and it is easy to see that the victim can be even a source of danger to his devourer. But in the very act of swallowing it is charged of necessity by the poison-apparatus with a most powerfully paralysing venom which speedily reduces it to a state of motionlessness, and so places it at the mercy of the gastric arrangements of its enemy. The

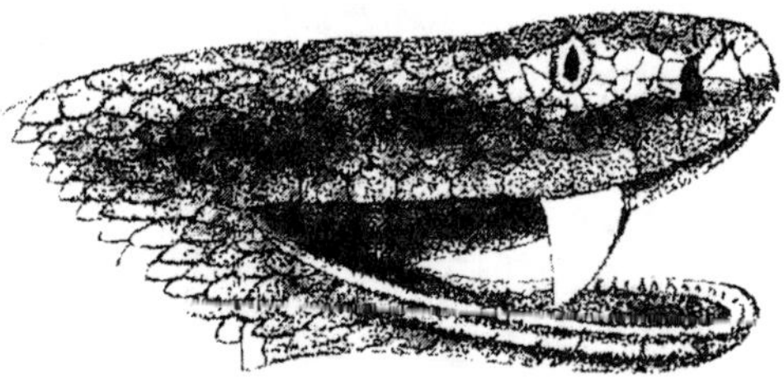

Head of Daboia Russellii.

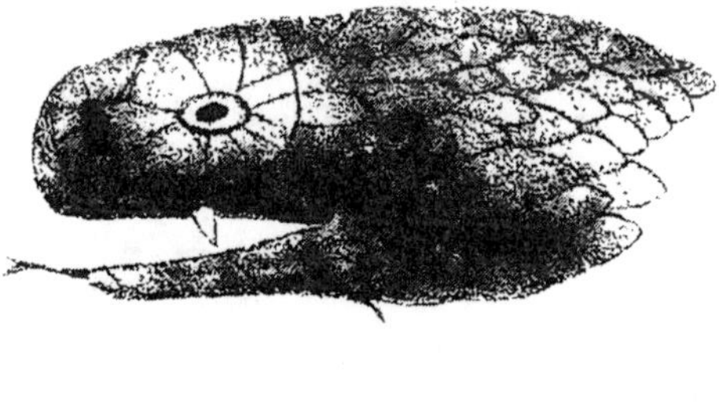

Head of Naja Tripudians (Cobra).

fang of the cobra is comparatively small, and the object to be poisoned must be well within the grasp of the jaws before the poison can be injected; thus the prey must be securely caught before it can be poisoned. It is true that all the varieties of the cobra have not exactly the same habits; but, of course, habits are infinitely more capable of alteration than structures.

The daboia, on the other hand, is a dreader of water; seldom, indeed, can it be induced to enter it, and I am not sure that in a state of nature it ever drinks it. It will live for months without touching it, though it is constantly offered. Its favourite food seems to be small mammals, lizards, and even birds. With its large fangs, easily movable and capable of protrusion laterally quite out of the mouth, it is able to inflict wounds on animals that it has never had within its grasp. I have myself been scratched by the fang of a viper on a finger which I thought was at a safe distance; and here, perhaps, we get a glimpse of the reason why it is of advantage to the daboia to have a venom different from that of the cobra. For should the daboia but wound a small mammal or lizard in the slightest degree, escape is impossible; for in a few seconds the little animal must fall over in convulsions. Thus the viper has but to make one dart forward and wound his victim, and await with confidence the result. Full of significance in this direction is the fact that daboia-poison is very much less deadly to frogs than cobra-venom. The poison-apparatus of the daboia may be looked upon as an elaborate hunting weapon, as much so as the gun to the sportsman. There is, however, a refinement about the physiological contrivance that can either kill at once by convulsions, or after an interval by paralysis, or at a still more remote period by blood-poisoning, to which the mechanical appliance utterly fails to attain.

Though snake-poisons can thus, to a great extent, be grouped according to the structural classification of the snakes to which they belong, the evidence given shows that there are distinct minor differences, even between those closely allied. That these slight differences of nature are related to slight differences in aim, is highly probable; but to be in a position to prove this, would require a most intimate acquaintance with all the habits of these reptiles in their natural state.

CHAPTER V.

THE NATURE OF SNAKE-POISONS.

THERE is a well-defined limit beyond which pure chemical methods are useless in the investigation of poisons. Chemistry can, of course, easily demonstrate to what chemical group or family a complex body belongs, and it can, therefore, afford valuable information as to its affinities. By establishing analogies in this way, chemistry often guides us to the nature of the action of a given substance, in so far as it acts like other members of the same group. But chemical investigation cannot tell us why a substance brings about a physiological effect. Chemistry can teach us that quinine and strychnia belong to the group called alkaloids, and therefore both probably possess physiological properties; but it cannot show us why one has an effect on malarious fever, and the other causes motor nerve discharges. It would, therefore, not be reasonable to expect chemistry to give us any further information about snake-poison than to indicate the class of substance to which it belongs, and those agents which are most likely to effect alterations in it.

Cobra-poison, which may be conveniently taken as a type of snake-poisons, is a clear, transparent fluid, varying in colour from a yellow or straw tint to complete colourlessness. It has an acid reaction; its consistence varies from almost that of water to that of the denser portions of white of egg. Its specific gravity, too, has a wide margin of variation. Specimens taken from several cobras and mixed gave a specific gravity of 1·058. It has a very bitter taste, which is chiefly perceived along the margin of the tongue, and a faint sickly odour. Daboia-venom is, however, without the bitter taste. When cobra-poison is evaporated it loses from 50 to 75 per cent. of water, and a yellow substance easily pulverizable, resembling gum arabic or dried egg albumen, is left behind. This substance possesses all the physiological properties of cobra-poison, and it can be kept in this state for years. Examined microscopically, cobra-poison is found to consist of a perfectly structureless plasma, in which a few bodies are to be detected. These bodies vary much, but if the poison is taken from a very active, healthy, and vigorous cobra, and care be used to prevent the admixture of mucus from the mouth, the number of structures to be seen will be very few; whereas the poison of a cobra that

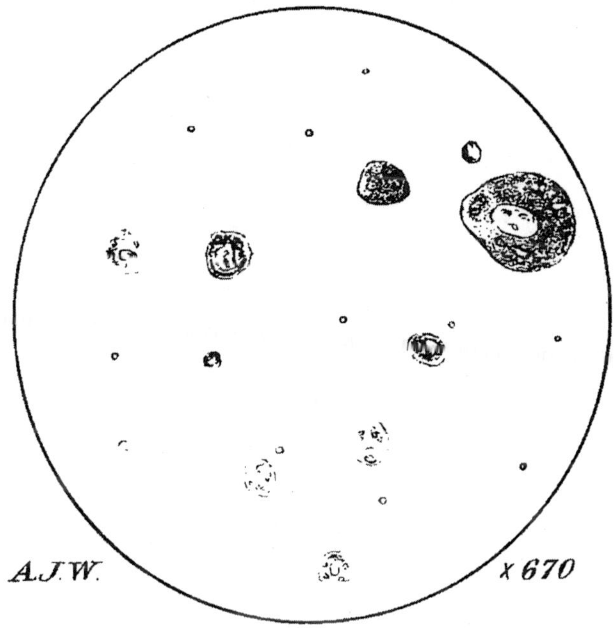

Structures found in the poison of the Naja Tripudians (Cobra)

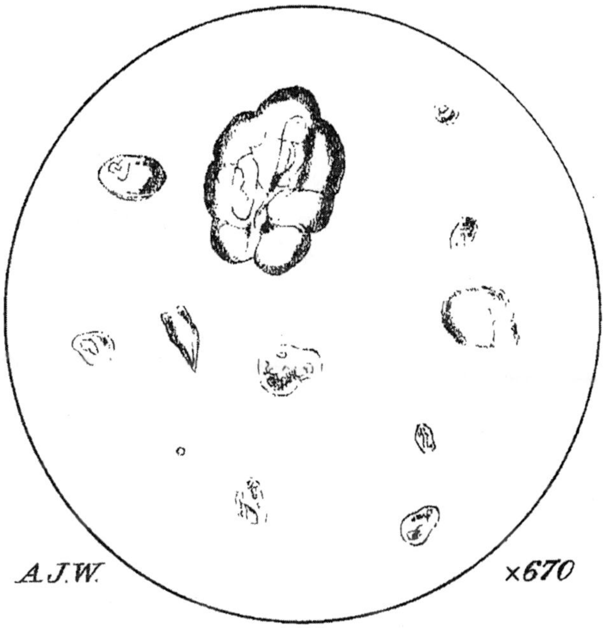

Structures found in the poison of the Daboia Russellii.

has been long in captivity and has been frequently handled will often contain numerous cells. But the purest and most active poison has but few structures in it. Sometimes a whole microscopic field may not present a single object. The structures usually seen are cells of different diameters, some of them clearly being epithelial cells from the mouth and lining membrane of the duct. Besides these there will be seen some much smaller very highly refracting bodies. The appearances of daboia-venom are similar. There is, then, nothing characteristic in the microscopic appearances of snake-poison, and the fact that the most active venom shows the fewest structures demonstrates that no importance is to be attached to those that are present.

The ultimate analysis of the poison by Dr. Armstrong gave the following percentage composition:—Carbon 45·76, nitrogen 14·3, hydrogen 6·6, sulphur 2·5.

When kept in the liquid state cobra-poison quickly becomes first neutral and then alkaline, and a few feathery and cubic crystals will form. If preserved in a loosely-corked test tube, it will become cloudy, smell offensively, and will swarm with bacteria in active movement, but it is still poisonous. The alkalinity now lessens, and the reaction becomes again acid, and the fluid then coagulates into a firm whitish opaque substance, somewhat like the coagulated white of egg, but of a lemon colour. If a small quantity of fluid is left uncoagulated it is poisonous, and the washings of the coagulum are also poisonous. When water is added to the coagulum decomposition rapidly sets in, and the products cannot be distinguished from those of any other similar organic body. The changes are greatly dependent on the physical conditions to which the poison is subjected. Coagulation occurred in some poison kept at 29° C. (84° F.) in ten days, whereas weeks were required when the temperature was 20° C. (68° F.)

The effects of heat on cobra-poison are well worthy of attention. It is well known that raising the temperature of a solution of cobra-poison to boiling point does not destroy its physiological effects, though much less local inflammation is then produced by it.

Experiment I.

Six centigrammes and a half of dried cobra-poison were heated in solution to boiling point, and the solution was afterwards injected into a dog.

12.50 P.M. Injection.
1.40 P.M. Retching.
1.45 P.M. Vomiting.
1.50 P.M. Staggering.
1.54 P.M. Muscular twitchings.
1.56 P.M. Profuse salivation ; cannot stand.
2.27½ P.M. Dead.

There was but very slight local inflammation at the site of the injection.

Here the venom killed with all the usual symptoms of cobra-poisoning.

When a solution of cobra-poison is heated to between 70° and 80° C. (158° to 176° F.), it first becomes cloudy and then a white precipitate falls. This precipitate, when washed, is not poisonous, and it corresponds in its behaviour exactly with albumen that has been coagulated in a similar manner. Moreover, if a small quantity of acetic acid be added previously to heating, no precipitate will fall, as is the case with albumen. But a solution of cobra-poison will withstand without injury a much higher temperature than 100° C.

Experiment II.

Five decigrammes (7·716 grains) of dried cobra-poison were dissolved in water. The solution measured ten cubic centimetres, and it was heated for thirty minutes under pressure to a temperature of 107° C. (224°·6 F.) One cubic centimetre of the solution (equalling five centigrammes or ·77 grain) was then injected into a fowl.

12.57 P.M. Injection.

1.13 P.M. Eye-lids closed; unable to stand; beak resting on the ground.

1.23 P.M. Convulsions.

1.27 P.M. Dead.

Here five centigrammes that had been heated in solution for half an hour to 107° C., killed a fowl in thirty minutes.

Experiment III.

The same solution that was used in the last experiment was again heated for another thirty minutes to the same temperature (107° C. or 224°·6 F.), and one cubic centimetre of it (containing five centigrammes or ·77 grain of the poison) afterwards injected into a fowl.

2.45 P.M. Injection.
3.55 P.M. Head drooping.
7.23 P.M. Convulsions.
7.35 P.M. Dead.

The same amount of poison, though heated for an hour to 107° C., in solution again killed with all the symptoms of cobra-poisoning. Now, though at the present time it would be difficult to say exactly what is or is not an infecting organism, or what the conditions of its vitality may be, yet little will be risked by stating that no life-possessing "germ" could possibly survive the treatment that the active agent of cobra-poison did in these experiments.

But there is evidence that a high temperature has some effect on the poison; for when the solution had been exposed to the heat for half an hour, five centigrammes took only thirty minutes to destroy life, whereas after an hour's exposure they required four hours and fifty minutes.

Experiment IV.

The same solution that had been used in the last two

experiments, and had been heated for an hour to 107° C. (225° F.) was again exposed for another hour to the same heat. One cubic centimetre of it was then injected into a fowl; but the bird, though kept for a long time under observation, never had any symptom of poisoning at all.

Here, then, after two hours' exposure in solution to a very high temperature, the poison was at last destroyed. But this destruction of the poisonous agent was gradual, the solution becoming weaker as the application of heat was continued.

There are, however, some other facts in connection with the effect of heat on cobra-poison that must be mentioned.

Experiment V.

A solution of dried cobra-poison was made, containing one centigramme (·154 grain) of poison in twenty cubic centimetres of water. One cubic centimetre of the solution, containing ·5 milligramme (·007 grain) of poison, killed a fowl in forty-two minutes; but this solution, after being heated for half an hour to 106° C. (222°·8 F.) was found to be completely harmless.

In this experiment a dilute solution of the poison was destroyed with comparative ease, whereas the solution used in the previous experiments, of 100 times the strength, resisted prolonged heat.

But it can be proved that even the heat of 100° C. has a distinct effect in diminishing the strength of a solution of cobra-poison. Thus half a cubic centimetre of dilute solution of cobra-poison, containing half a milligramme of poison, killed a small fowl in thirty-three minutes; whereas after the solution had been boiled, it took forty-seven minutes to kill a fowl of the same size.

Moreover, when a solution of cobra-poison, containing 2·5 milligrammes to the cubic centimetre was heated to 100° C. ·6 milligramme of the poison killed a fowl in sixty-four minutes, whereas when the solution which was heated only contained 1·25 milligrammes to the cubic centimetre, ·6 milligramme of the poison required no less than **111** minutes to cause death. This shows clearly with how much greater ease heat destroys dilute solutions than concentrated ones.

We see, then, that a temperature of 100° C. has a distinct effect in lessening the strength of a solution of cobra-poison, but that a very great heat continued for a very long time is required to completely destroy the properties of a concentrated solution. If cobra-poison consisted of a collection of "germs," it is, of course, conceivable that the "germs" might resist great heat, but it is not credible that one collection of them should be destroyed by heating for half an hour to 106° (Experiment V.), whilst another should resist for more than an hour a heat of 107° C. (Experiments II. and III.) The heat that would destroy one germ would destroy all, and the solution, instead of gradually becoming weaker, would at once lose its virulence with the death of its poison-bearing agents. But it is thoroughly in accordance with experience that dilute solutions of chemical agents should be decomposed with greater ease than concentrated ones, and this decomposition would proceed gradually as the heat was continued. The whole evidence, therefore, that is given by the action of heat is strongly in favour of cobra-poison being a chemical agent of very great stability of constitution.

In the chapter on daboia-poison it was shown that if that poison be heated to 100° C. it loses all power of causing convulsions; but this is not the whole of the case, for if the poison be heated only to 80° C. (176° F.) the same effect is produced. This change is not due to the precipitation of albumen, for it occurs if this is prevented by adding acetic acid, nor is it due to the volatilization of any constituent of the poison, for the products obtained in a receiver connected with the heated solution, and kept at 0° C., were not poisonous, but it seems to depend on the destruction of a highly organised, easily decomposed agent, for the addition of nitric acid diluted with its own bulk of water also destroyed it. There can be no doubt, therefore, that it is a separate component of the poison, as after its destruction the paralysis-producing power is still present in the solution. Taken together with the fact that the daboia has an additional gland on its poison duct, it would seem to be a highly elaborated constituent added to the paralysing agent to discharge some special function.

In investigating the nature of snake-poison, it is not only necessary to note what physical changes the venom undergoes when treated with re-agents, but, what is more important to observe, any alteration in its physiological effects after it has been subjected to any chemical process. It is more to this latter method that we must look for light as to the constitution of the poisonous agent, as the substance itself can only be recognised by its effects.

The first group of substances that would be naturally selected to ascertain the effect on cobra-poison, are the agents termed antiseptic. To enable, as far as possible, a comparison to be made as to their relative effects, in each case the same amount of poison was used, and it was exposed to the action of an equal quantity of each of the re-agents for the same time under the same physical conditions. As, however, some of the agents were gaseous, is was not always possible to use the same quantity of substance. The agents chosen were carbolic acid, ferrous sulphate, potassium permanganate, sodium hyposulphite, zinc chloride, sulphurous acid, and chlorine. The method employed was the following:—One centigramme ('154 grain) of the dried poison was dissolved in one cubic centimetre of water. To this was added one cubic centimetre of water, which contained five centigrammes ('77 grain) of the re-agent, the effect of which it was desired to ascertain. The mixture was then hermetically closed in a glass tube and allowed to remain for twenty hours, and the solution was then tested physiologically. In the case of gaseous disinfectants, one cubic centimetre of the officinal solutions of these gases were used. The following are the times that the mixed solutions required to cause death in fowls :—

One centigramme (·154 grain) of cobra-poison alone, twenty minutes.

With sodium hyposulphite, twenty-four minutes.

With carbolic acid, thirty-six minutes.

With ferrous sulphate, forty-six minutes.

With solution of chlorine, fifty-three minutes.

With solution of sulphurous acid, sixty-five minutes.

With zinc chloride, ninety minutes.

With permanganate of potash, caused no symptom.

In this list it is seen that in every case there was some retardation of the symptoms, ferrous sulphate, chlorine, sulphurous oxide, zinc chloride, each producing considerable weakening of the poison. Carbolic acid caused very slight delay, and its use was attended with its own special toxic symptoms. In no other case was there the least change in the nature of the symptoms. By only one re-agent—namely, potassium permanganante—was the poison completely destroyed.

It is a very significant fact that whereas carbolic acid, which is peculiarly destructive to bacteria and to lowly organisms, and has great efficacy in preventing their appearance, only caused very slight retardation, that on the other hand potassium permanganate, which has great powers of oxidation when placed in organic solutions, rendered the poison harmless. When a solution of cobra-poison is mixed with a solution of potassium permanganate, a considerable rise of temperature immediately takes place—as much as five or six degrees centigrade (9° to 10°·8 F.) being often noticed. This is, of course, a sign of great chemical activity; the solution becomes thick and of a dark brown colour. A very great impairment of its physiological properties is at once observed. But so sensitive are birds to the least trace of unchanged cobra-venom that the poison must be kept exposed to the action of the permanganate for a very considerable time before the whole of the poison is completely decomposed.

As it was found that potassium permanganate does destroy the poison, steps were taken to see if it would be of any practical use in the treatment of animals suffering from snake-bite. It was found by experiment that a considerable quantity of potassium permanganate, dissolved in a weak saline solution, could be injected into the circulation of an animal without producing any immediate effect. A dog, therefore, was taken suffering from cobra-poison. Through a cannula, placed in its saphena vein, a saline solution of permanganate of potash was injected; but though a large quantity of the antiseptic was cautiously and gradually introduced into the circulation, and though at the same time life was prolonged by artificial respiration, in no way was the least benefit to be perceived from the remedy. The reason is obvious. It is quite true that potassium permanganate destroys the active agent of cobra-venom, by oxidizing it; but when introduced into the blood it, of course, commences oxidizing indifferently all the organic matters with which it comes in contact, but it has no power of selecting one organic substance for oxidation rather than another. The oxidizing power of the permanganate is, therefore, exerted on the constituents of the blood generally, instead of being reserved for the cobra-poison in it alone. So, if cobra-poison is dissolved in an organic solution, and the permanganate is added before injection, the poison suffers little, if any, diminution of strength, for the oxidation has taken place chiefly at the expense of the other organic matter. Thus it would be necessary to destroy all the constituents of the blood by oxidation, before all the poison in it could be destroyed too. If a substance should be found having the power of oxidation, with a special affinity for exercising it on snake-poison, the problem of the treatment of snake-bite would be solved; but potassium permanganate has not this special power.

There is, besides potassium permanganate, a large

class of substances which also have the power of rendering cobra-poison inert. It is the class of metallic salts capable of precipitating albumen. The following experiment gives an instance in point.

Experiment VI.

To one-tenth of a cubic centimetre of distilled water, containing one milligramme of dried cobra-poison, was added one cubic centimetre of a solution of silver nitrate containing five centigrammes (·77 grain) of the silver salt. After the solutions had been thoroughly mixed, they were injected into a fowl. No symptom whatever followed.

To this class belongs gold chloride, mercuric chloride, and many similar bodies. The only essential conditions to observe are that the salt should be in great excess of the poison, and that time should be allowed for the whole precipitate to form.

But other bodies, also capable of precipitating albumen, have the same destructive effect as these metallic salts. If to a solution of cobra-poison tannic acid be added till no further precipitate can be thrown down, the resultant fluid has no physiological effect.

Various statements have been made by different observers about the action of alcohol on snake-poison. The following are the chief results:—If to a solution of cobra-poison absolute alcohol be added, a white precipitate is thrown down. After the precipitate has been thoroughly washed with alcohol, it can be re-dissolved in water, and the solution produces all the effects of cobra-poison. If dried cobra-poison, in a state of fine powder, be added to absolute alcohol, and the mixture be frequently agitated, the alcohol will derive no poisonous property from the cobra-poison. If, however, instead of absolute alcohol, rectified spirit be employed, the water in the rectified spirit is capable of taking up a certain amount of the poison. So, if absolute alcohol be added to liquid cobra-poison as it comes from the snake, a precipitate will fall which is poisonous; but the supernatant fluid is also poisonous from some of the active agent being held in solution by the natural fluid of the venom. That this is so, can be proved by evaporating this clear supernatant fluid to a small bulk, when a further addition of absolute alcohol will produce a further precipitate of the poisonous agent. In other words, the active agent of cobra-poison is precipitated by, and is totally insoluble in, absolute alcohol; but mixtures of alcohol and water are capable of dissolving a certain amount of the poison in proportion to the quantity of water present. As a method of treatment, alcohol is useless, except in so far as it is administered on general principles as a stimulant.

Carbolic acid, as has been shown, has some effect in delaying and lessening the action of cobra-poison when mixed with it, probably by decomposing some of it; for the longer it remains in contact with the poison before injection, the greater is the diminution of strength.

But, administered independently of the poison, it has no effect whatever.

Sulphuric and nitric acid have no action on the poison, except they are added in sufficient strength to cause actual destruction of the organic matter.

Ammonia neither diminishes the strength of a solution of cobra-poison, nor lengthens life if given separately.

Perhaps the class of agents from the actions of which we can learn most about the nature of cobra-poison is that of the fixed alkalies, though very many contradictory statements have been made on this subject.

Experiment VII.

One decigramme (1·54 grain) of dried cobra-poison was dissolved in three cubic centimetres of the officinal solution of potash, and the solution was injected into a fowl, but the bird never had the slightest symptom of poisoning.

In this experiment it is shown that cobra-poison dissolved in a solution of potash has no effect. In repeating it, two points must be borne in mind; one is, that the solution should not be made hastily, and the other is, that the solution of potash should be pure. At the high temperature at which chemical re-agents are necessarily kept in India, solution of potash rapidly takes up carbonic acid. In India it may be said that liquor potassæ is merely a solution of potassic carbonate. In all the experiments made with this re-agent, the solutions were specially prepared for the purpose.

But it can be proved that though cobra-poison, when mixed with a caustic alkali, produces no symptoms, yet it has not permanently lost its poisonous properties, as they can be restored to it.

Experiment VIII.

A quantity of fresh cobra-poison from several cobras was taken. It was found that one quarter of a cubic centimetre of this poison killed a dog in sixty-one minutes.

Two cubic centimetres of the poison were taken, and to them were added two cubic centimetres of a solution of potash, containing one gramme of the alkali in six cubic centimetres. Two cubic centimetres of the resulting mixture (containing one cubic centimetre of the fresh poison) were then injected into a dog, but the animal never experienced a symptom of poisoning.

Two cubic centimetres of the mixed solution of potash and cobra-poison still remained. To these were added two cubic centimetres of the officinal solution of acetic acid, and one cubic centimetre of the mixed solutions containing one quarter of a cubic centimetre of the original poison was injected into a dog. This animal had all the symptoms of cobra-poisoning, and died in one hour and fifty-six minutes.

Thus we see that cobra-poison mixed with a solution of potash can be injected into the system without producing any symptom, but that when acetic acid is added to this solution all the powers of the poison are restored.

That this change is not due to the fact that the solution is rendered alkaline, can be shown by adding ammonia, when no alteration in the symptoms is produced, and also by the circumstance that it is not necessary to completely neutralise the alkali by the acid to restore the activity to the poison.

More light is thrown on the nature of this change by the following experiments.

Experiment IX.

Twelve centigrammes (about two grains) of dried cobra-poison were dissolved in a solution of caustic potash; after standing for eighteen hours, the solution was neutralised with acetic acid, and a white flocculent precipitate fell. A fowl, into which this neutralised solution was injected, died with all the symptoms of cobra-poisoning, though they were induced but slowly.

Experiment X.

One cubic centimetre of fresh cobra-poison was mixed with four cubic centimetres of the potash solution, and the mixture was allowed to stand for twenty-four hours. It was then neutralised with acetic acid, but no precipitate fell. The resulting solution had no poisonous properties whatever.

Thus, after standing exposed to the action of the alkali for eighteen hours, the strength of the poison was greatly impaired, and after twenty-four hours it had permanently lost all poisonous properties.

The rapidity of this change can be greatly aided by a high temperature. This loss of power is found to be accompanied by a physical change; for when the solution is no longer poisonous, acetic acid fails to throw down any longer a white precipitate. Now this white flaky precipitate gives the characteristic albuminoid re-action with Millon's re-agent. It is reasonable, therefore, to conclude, that as long as the poisonous agent of cobra-venom is capable of recognition chemically as albumen, so long is it poisonous, and no longer. Now, potash is a well-known agent for decomposing albumen, and is the ordinary means for preparing leucin and other derivatives from it. When, therefore, cobra-poison is circulating in the system, mixed with the alkali, the chemical agent is occupied in decomposing it, and thus cobra-venom, instead of producing those changes in the constituents of the body which are necessary for its power of destruction, is, in its turn, itself being destroyed. It is much to be regretted that, introduced separately to the poison, potash has, like potassic permanganate, no power of specially selecting cobra-poison for its destructive action. It is, however, a point of deep interest in general pathology, that a class of substances that can produce constitutional effects after sometimes prolonged incubation, can be demonstrated to belong to the group of bodies called albuminoid.

CHAPTER VI.

SOME PRACTICAL CONSIDERATIONS CONNECTED WITH THE SUBJECT OF SNAKE-POISONING, ESPECIALLY REGARDING PREVENTION AND TREATMENT.

As there is no agent at present known that can counteract the effects of snake-poison when introduced into the system, it will be seen that it is of the highest importance to prevent any of the poison entering the circulation. As long as the poison remains at the spot where it is injected by the snake, it is harmless. It is only when it enters the circulation that it is capable of doing injury. The exact position of the poison deposited by the snake is, therefore, worthy of careful study. When a snake obtains a fair hold of his victim both fangs—one on each side of the upper jaw—pierce the skin, and the poison is injected through each. There are thus, beneath the skin, two separate deposits of venom, from which absorption takes place simultaneously. Death, therefore, as a rule, is quicker in cases of the natural bite, than after the artificial injection of the poison in one place. In the case of the cobra, if the bite has been inflicted on a fairly plane surface, as the ball of the thumb, or the dorsum of the foot, the distance between the punctures will be, as a rule, seventeen millimetres, rarely exceeding twenty, or going below fifteen millimetres; or, roughly, about seven-tenths of an inch, and varying from three-fifths to four-fifths of an inch. As the skin is movable, and penetration by both fangs may not occur simultaneously, there may be a difference in the distance between the two punctures, due to this cause. The punctures may or may not be visible to the naked eye. Sometimes their site is marked by a few drops of blood or serum exuding; or there may be a scratch, if the victim has withdrawn the part rapidly. Should the snake not have been interrupted, on examining the part with a lens the punctures will be seen. They may be either short, straight cuts, gaping slightly at the centre, or triangular punctures, the area of the triangle being the pit into which the fang has been forced. The difference seems to depend on whether the snake has made a hasty dart and rapid withdrawal, or whether it was a deliberate and prolonged bite.

The poison is deposited at a depth below the punctures of about three or four millimetres; it may be more if the fang is able to depress the skin at the spot. The poison, also, is not deposited in the skin itself, but in the areolar tissue beneath; and this is a point of importance, for, as the skin is freely movable over the parts below, especially on the back of the hands and feet, the fang may have dragged the skin away from its proper position before injecting the poison, so that the poison deposit may not be immediately beneath the punctures.

The first consideration to be attended to in dealing with a case of snake-bite is at once to prevent any more poison being absorbed from the deposits. All other considerations must yield to this. A minute or two may make all the difference between life and death. Therefore nothing else is to be thought of till any further absorption of the poison is rendered impossible. Fortunately there is a practical point in connection with snake-bite that gives us a clear indication of how to proceed in the majority of cases in the first instance. The best series of cases of snake-bite in the human subject, is contained in Sir J. Fayrer's "Thanatophidia." In the list given there, fifty-four instances are detailed, in which the exact spot bitten is specified. From this the following table has been prepared:—

Place of bite.	Percentage of total cases.
Fingers and wrist ...	31·48
Fore-arm	1·85
Elbow	5·56
Shoulder	1·85
Feet, toes, and ankle ...	48·15
Leg	3·70
Thigh	1·85

Place of bite.			Percentage of total cases.
Breast	...	...	1·85
Ear ...	...	...	1·85
Perineum	...	...	1·85

In other words, 94·54 per cent. of persons bitten are wounded on the extremities, and it is, therefore, possible to withdraw at once the part bitten from the circulation, without injuring the person in the slightest degree. There is only one way of doing this effectually. At once let a thick india-rubber band—such as is used in Esmarch's bandage for bloodless operations—be firmly bound on the limb above the part bitten. No circulation, and, therefore, no absorption can go on after this; and time can be taken to consider what further proceedings are necessary. An ordinary cord or string, or bandage, is nearly useless compared with the india-rubber band. I have known fatal absorption take place when a string has been applied so tightly as actually to cut the flesh, and apparently strangulate the limb completely, causing acute suffering, evidently from the cord not accommodating itself accurately to the form of the member, and thus leaving a small channel for the circulation. The india-rubber band is nearly painless, and properly applied is an absolute safeguard against further absorption. An ordinary piece of cord or string is commonly recommended as the proper application. It is, as I have said, of very slight use indeed, and then only when applied so as to be equivalent to amputation.

But, of course, as an india-rubber band is seldom accessible, recourse must often be had to its nearly useless substitute. But the india-rubber cord is so inexpensive, so easily applied, and so completely fulfils its purpose of preventing further absorption of the poison, and thus placing the patient in a position of complete safety for the time, and it is of so much importance that it should be applied as quickly as possible after the bite, that I cannot but think that every tháná, as well as every dispensary, in districts where deaths from snake-bite are common, should have one, and that the officials should be instructed how to apply it properly. I think it would not be going too far to express a belief that European households, and those of the upper classes of natives in the same districts, should also be provided with so simple means for the immediate treatment of snake-bite.

The india-rubber band should be firmly and tightly bound round the extremity above the seat of injury, and should encircle the limb several times, and it should be applied in all cases as soon as possible after the receipt of the injury. The patient having thus been secured against any further absorption of the poison, time is allowed for treatment.

The surgeon's first care should be to ascertain if the patient has been really poisoned; for the most venomous snakes may bite, and yet, from their poison-apparatus having been exhausted on some object previously, they may not inject one particle of poison. Symptoms are almost useless as an indication, as the most profound collapse may be caused by the fear of impending death, when the reptile causing the dread has not been in the least poisonous; and the victim not seldom does not see his assailant at all. Amputations, ending fatally, have even been performed on persons who have thus apparently had symptoms of snake-poisoning, though it has been proved afterwards that the snake was a harmless one. Moreover, when the time for symptoms has come, the time for treatment has passed. It will be seen, therefore, of how great importance it is to ascertain whether the person has been poisoned as well as bitten.

It was pointed out in the chapter on cobra-poisoning that snake-poison produces at once inflammation at the spot where it has been injected. The degree of inflammation may vary greatly, depending partly on the species of snake, partly on the amount of poison injected and the time it has remained in the tissues, and partly on the position where it has been injected. Of Indian snakes the daboia produces the greatest amount of inflammation, and the Bungarus cœruleus or krait, I think, the least. Now this inflammation is not at all perceptible on the surface of the skin. After applying the band, the first thing to be done by the surgeon is to make a free incision through the skin at the site of the bite, and reflect back the skin on each side, so as to get a complete view of the underlying tissue. Now, it is clear that if no venom has been injected by a poisonous snake, or if the bite has been given by a harmless reptile or mammal, no subjacent inflammation can be present. A bite by a mongoose or Lycodon can produce nothing but a mechanical puncture. But if inflammation is present, it is evident that there must be some reason for it, and the only cause that can produce such rapid inflammation of the subcutaneous areolar tissue under these circumstances is snake-poison. There are, of course, wide differences in the appearances to be seen in the areolar tissue under the skin, in the neighbourhood of the bite. In the case of the daboia a deep purple patch will be found at the spot, whereas the Bungarus cœruleus or krait will only cause a pale slight watery exudation, not much in quantity, and of a faint pink hue. The cobra, which is the snake that chiefly concerns us, always leaves decided marks of its poison, unless the venom has been thrown directly into a vein, when, of course, treatment is useless if sufficient to kill has been injected. It must be borne in mind that if any change whatever is found in the areolar tissue we must conclude that poison is present, and act accordingly; for we can only find out by leaving the patient alone and seeing if death supervene, if sufficient poison to kill has been injected; and this, of course, is an utterly unjustifiable proceeding. Every opportunity should be taken to become thoroughly acquainted with the appearance of areolar tissue, both in health and under the influence of the presence of snake-poison, as mistakes may easily be made from ignorance of the appearances presented.

The next step is to remove the whole of the deposited poison. Many proposals have been made from time to time on this subject. Suction, burning, igniting gunpowder on the spot, excision, &c. &c., have been recommended. But, practically, all methods must yield to the careful dissection out with a knife of all the parts likely to contain the poison. It is not of the least use pinching up the skin and excising it, as the skin never contains the poison at all, and the areolar tissue holding the poison would retract before the knife and be left behind. The following is the only efficient way:—An incision at least an inch and a half long should be made through the site of the bite; the skin should then be excised on each side for three-quarters of an inch. This will freely expose the parts below. The skin should be reflected back in every direction by the scalpel, and with a forceps the whole of the areolar tissue underneath should be thoroughly and completely dissected out, going freely up the limb in the direction of the returning blood-current. On the ball of the thumb, not only the areolar tissue, but the deep fascia and some of the muscle beneath should be removed, as the fang is capable of sinking in especially deeply here. On the fingers and toes all the tissues should be cut away at the site of the bite till the bone is reached, and, if necessary, on the back of the hand or foot, tendon and every structure may be cleared right down to the bone. Every part that may contain the poison must be removed. Life is not to be saved by a haphazard cutting away of anything that comes first, but by an intelligent and careful dissecting away of the parts holding the poison, bearing in mind the anatomical peculiarities of each region. On the surface of the limbs it will be enough, as a rule, to remove freely the subcutaneous tissue, especially if this be thick. The skin should in all cases be removed over an area of an inch and a half square. It need scarcely be remarked that amputation is totally unnecessary, as excision answers every purpose; but if it is found requisite to remove all the soft parts from one of the less prominent fingers or toes, it may be perhaps to the patient's advantage to remove that finger or toe completely. Careful but free excision, guided by the appearance of the parts, is all that is necessary; but it should be remembered that any shortcoming in carrying out the excision may result in the death of the patient. It would be cruel leniency to leave any tissue, however important, that served as a receptacle for the poison. After the whole of the suspected parts have been thoroughly dissected out, the india-rubber band may be removed, but not till then, the part having first been freely washed with a solution of caustic potash or potassic permanganate.

It may be urged that the appearances of the inflammation produced by snake-poison may lead one to excise the bitten part, even when sufficient poison has not been injected to kill. This may be true, but the injury inflicted is trifling compared with the fearful risk that would be run by leaving the patient alone. Summed up shortly, the position is this:—If we do not consult the condition of the parts we shall be absolutely without any guide at all, and must act by guess-work, or wait till the symptoms have developed, when interference is useless. But by consulting the appearance of the parts we shall obtain information, the accuracy of which will be in proportion to our knowledge of the subject.

In those rare cases where the victim is bitten on the body, all that can be done is to make, as quickly as possible, a complete excision of the part. It is singular that out of the few cases that do occur on the trunk, in a large proportion of them the wound is on a place where complete excision can be performed with ease, namely, the ear, the breast, and the scrotum. The reason appears to be that a snake has some difficulty in seizing hold of any part of the body which presents a smooth flat surface, but that any pendulous part can be grasped without difficulty by the reptile. This is a fact much in the favour of this class of victims.

That these proceedings are of the greatest practical use, and are quite sufficient under ordinary circumstances, the following cases will prove.

A native woman was brought into the Presidency Hospital, Calcutta, by her friends, who stated she had put her hand into a dark corner of her house to reach something, when she was bitten in the hand by a snake. There was a distinct mark of a wound on the knuckle, and she herself was in such profound collapse as to be almost pulseless and quite speechless. An incision through the skin at the wound revealed the fact that the underlying tissue was perfectly normal. Her friends were told that there was no danger, and in a short time she walked out of the hospital perfectly well.

On another occasion a young man, a pure European, was admitted, having been bitten, whilst in his compound, by a snake on the finger. A tight ligature had been applied to the arm soon after the bite, and this was replaced at once by an india-rubber band. An incision revealed extensive areolar inflammation, and a free excision was at once performed, but only enough to secure safety, as the subsequent sloughing from the effect of the poison showed. He ultimately completely recovered.

The great advantage of the india-rubber ligature is that it gives time for the patient to be removed to where he can obtain proper attention, and also affords opportunity to the surgeon for consideration and deliberate action. That no further absorption can go on after this form of ligature is properly applied, the following experiment will show.

Experiment I.

A dog was bitten on the leg by a vigorous cobra.

2.15 P.M. Bitten.

2.17 P.M. A ligature of india-rubber applied above the bitten part.

3.16 P.M. The part containing the poison carefully dissected out.

3.20 P.M. Ligature removed.

The dog recovered completely, having suffered only slightly from the effects of the poison.

Here, two minutes after the dog was bitten the ligature was applied, but no further steps were taken for one hour, and yet the dog was saved; and if the interval between the application of the ligature and excision had been prolonged to a day, the result would have been the same. After the poison-bearing tissue had been dissected out, it was steeped in water, and the resulting fluid injected into a fowl, which died rapidly from cobra-poisoning, showing that there was abundant poison in the tissue to destroy life, if it could only have entered the circulation.

It is difficult to say what are the limits of time at which the ligature may be usefully applied, as it depends on so many various circumstances. If the fang of the snake should chance to have entered a vein and thus the poison have been thrown directly into the circulation, as certainly happens sometimes, it is clear that no ligature can avail anything, as the poison is already in the blood. In another extreme case in the other direction, the poison may only have been injected in just sufficient quantity to destroy life, in a part far removed from active vitality, perhaps in a person with languid circulation ; say on the dorsal surface of one of the toes. Under these circumstances it would be long before the whole of the poison would be absorbed, and anything short of total absorption would fail to destroy life. Here there would be a long interval during which the application of the ligature would be useful. As the exact circumstances of a bite can never be known it is right in all cases to apply the ligature at once, and never to hesitate as to whether it will be useful or not. A very short hesitation may cost the patient's life, and as no injury is caused by its application, there can be no question as to the expediency of applying it in all cases as soon as possible after the infliction of the wound. And it is of great desirability that the excision should also follow speedily.

It may be asked, considering there are several substances that destroy snake-poison—such as certain metallic salts, tannic acid, potassic hydrate, and potassic permanganate—why should not these substances be used in preference to excision. The reply is obvious. If we could know the exact position of the poison, and if there were only one deposit we might possibly succeed in destroying it by injection. But to remove the poison deposited by the bite of a snake requires a most intelligent dissection, guided by eye-sight and judgment, but an injection of a chemical agent must be to a great extent made by guess-work; and the solution, instead of following the poison, takes the line of least resistance in the tissues, often leading it far from the poison. Applying the agent to an incision over the wound is also nearly useless. In cases where the poison has been artificially injected by an instrument, I have obtained excellent results both with potassic hydrate, sodic hydrate, and potassic permanganate; but after the natural bite of a snake this method of treatment is without avail. By chance it may occasionally succeed, but though I have had special instruments contrived so as to irrigate the whole of the poisoned area with these re-agents, I have, in a very large proportion of cases, failed altogether; whereas with thorough excision under the condition that sufficient poison to kill has not already been absorbed, failure is impossible. All that chemical agents can do is to destroy the tissue and the poison in it, and by no means can you tell whether you are destroying more than is necessary, or less. But with excision you remove exactly the poison deposit. You are guided by sight and knowledge. In the artificial injection of the poison through a tube, the re-agent follows through that tube the course taken by the poison—a piece of simplicity of practice which unfortunately does not obtain after cobra-bite.

After the tissue bearing the poison has, as far as possible, been removed, advantage undoubtedly can be obtained by using either potassic hydrate or potassic permanganate to the wound, and they should, if used, be applied in solutions of considerable strength. Perhaps potassic hydrate is the best agent, but it should be applied in as strong a solution as can be obtained, and it should be used to the tissues above and around the wound, especially in the direction of the returning blood-current. It should be remembered that liquor potassæ is never in India more than a solution of potassic carbonate, and therefore a fresh solution of the solid re-agent should be made.

Sucking the wound inflicted by the snake is completely useless. A fair idea of its efficacy can be obtained by attempting to remove a hypodermic injection of morphia by suction.

When the symptoms of snake-poisoning have once developed, a condition of appalling gravity is produced, of which little that is hopeful can be said here. The patient will sooner or later present symptoms of advancing paralysis. Now nothing can be clearer in the case of animals than the evidence that anything that disturbs the victim or excites his circulation hastens the development of this state. In administering remedies to animals suffering from snake-poisoning, nothing is more conspicuous than the fact that the more frequent or the more exciting the administration of the antidote is, the shorter is the duration of life after it. The patient, therefore, should be kept quiet and his strength husbanded. Nourishing food should be given if necessary, and if there is any tendency to syncope a small amount of stimulants. In animals, however, alcohol certainly does not lengthen life.

If the bite has been inflicted by a colubrine snake, salivation and paralysis of the tongue and throat will soon show themselves. The head should be placed on one side to allow the saliva to trickle out, as otherwise it will probably enter the paralysed larynx, and aid the process of suffocation; the tongue, also, should be prevented from falling back, and at this stage the patient should have nothing given him to swallow, as he is quite incapable of doing so, and therefore the substance will very likely be forced into the windpipe. I have even found, after death, remedies in the air-tubes in the lungs, which had been forced there by the anxious friends, a circumstance which would have rendered recovery impossible.

The next feature will be failure of the respiratory power. In the most acute form this occurs in a very rapid manner, the function appearing to be suddenly overpowered, but it is not always thus extinguished. In the less rapid cases the respiration fails very gradually, and as death is clearly the result of this failure every effort should be made to stimulate the lessening function. Frequently repeated affusions of cold water on the face, whilst the rest of the body is kept dry and warm, have a marked effect in keeping the function alive, also artificial respiration. In regard to the uses of artificial respiration in snake-poisoning, it may be said that though it can never restore function to a paralysed respiratory centre, yet it can undoubtedly ward off, for a time at least, that paralysis. When natural respiration has failed, it is useless to resort to artificial, for though most of the functions of life may be maintained for a considerable time, yet the natural respiratory action does not return. But when only just sufficient poison has been absorbed to impair the respiratory function, so that complete cessation is just threatened, artificial respiration, when resorted to *before the function has ceased,* may enable the crisis to be surmounted till the effects of the poison have somewhat passed off; so that the natural respiration, though very slight, and not of itself sufficient to support life, may be maintained till the natural power has returned. The following is a case in point:—

Experiment II.

A pariah dog, on whom tracheotomy had been performed a day or two previously, had one cubic centimetre of fresh cobra-poison injected subcutaneously.

12.30 P.M. Injection.

12.33 P.M. Thirty cubic centimetres of solution of caustic potash, containing one gramme of the alkali to six cubic centimetres of water, was injected through the cannula of the syringe which had not been removed.

12.45 P.M. Salivation.

4.15 P.M. Not able to stand. Respiration very faint. Artificial respiration by bellows and cannula through the tracheal opening commenced.

5.3 P.M. Breathing by artificial respiration almost entirely.

5.50 P.M. Natural respiration stronger.

6.10 P.M. Artificial respiration stopped, as the natural was sufficient to support life.

10.10 P.M. Able to get off couch and walk about.

The animal completely recovered.

Here, through the alkali having been injected through the same channel as the poison, and soon after it, but a small quantity of poison was absorbed, artificial respiration was resorted to before natural respiration had stopped and only to aid it. The artificial respiration was constantly interrupted, to see that the natural respiration was still performed, so that all that was done was to assist the failing respiratory powers, not to supersede them, and the animal's life was saved. A result like this cannot be often looked for under the natural conditions of poisoning, as every detail was here arranged beforehand. Great importance must be attached to the fact that the tracheotomy was performed previously. But the case shows that every effort should be made to assist the failing respiratory powers. When natural respiration, however, has completely ceased, though the circulation can be maintained for a long time by using artificial respiration, I have never seen the least return of the natural function, though I have tried perseveringly, both in cobra and daboia poisoning. All our efforts, therefore, must be directed to maintaining and aiding the natural function, as this, once completely extinguished, cannot be restored. Artificial respiration by bellows and tracheal cannula is far superior to mere movement of the arms. But in resorting to artificial respiration care should be taken not to overdo it. Thirty strokes a minute is the extreme limit that should be reached.

After all, we can but seldom hope to achieve much by any method after the symptoms have appeared, yet cold affusion and artificial respiration by the Sylvester plan of moving the arms, a little advantage may be gained in the slighter cases. The other method referred to requires too elaborate arrangements to be often available.

In regard to remedies, though I have tried with care every one that has been brought to my notice, and they have been very numerous, it is impossible to exaggerate the uselessness of each of them.

In the prolonged cases of viperine poisoning, where symptoms of hæmorrhage supervene, it is usual for them to appear within six or eight hours after the infliction of the bite. This condition is most serious, death usually resulting, even though it may be as late as the second week. But recoveries have been recorded even in severe cases, showing that no change incompatible with life has occurred. It is evident, from the history of these cases that death is due to the loss of blood, and it would therefore be clearly the indication to prevent a fatal result from this cause to transfuse from time to time a small quantity of fresh blood to replace that which has escaped from the vessels. The great muscular weakness which is developed in acute cases of viperine poisoning, affecting especially the heart, would render any attempt to make the patient exert himself especially dangerous.

In the chronic form of poisoning seen after the bite of the Bungarus fasciatus, nothing at present can be said as to its treatment, though every effort should be made to support the strength of the victim. But the fact of its occurrence so long after the receipt of the injury adds much weight to what has already been urged as to the importance of early and complete excision of the wounded part in all cases of poisonous snake-bite.

Closely connected with the subject of treatment is the nature of the means that can be employed to prevent loss of life in India from snake-poisoning. Foremost stands the possibility of destroying the noxious reptiles themselves, and the use of rewards in aiding this process; and as different opinions are held on this subject it may be advisable to review the arguments that may be employed. Against the system of granting rewards it may be urged—(1.) That the number of poisonous snakes in the country is so enormous that it is practically impossible to lessen them if the whole revenue of India be used for the purpose. (2.) That the snakes chiefly inhabit the jungles, where it is very difficult to attack them, and that it is only when natives go into out-of-the-way places that they incur the risk of being bitten. (3.) That the practice of giving rewards for capturing snakes, instead of diminishing the number of snakes would tend to increase them, as men would take to breeding snakes for the rewards instead of catching them.

The number of snakes in India must, in truth, be enormous, but we have no grounds for forming the slightest idea as to what their number may be, and therefore there is no evidence, one way or the other, whether they can be exterminated or not. Large sums have been disbursed in certain districts with little effect, but in other cases a distinct diminution in mortality has occurred. But it should be stated that often large amounts have been disbursed without any safeguard as to whether the reward was given for poisonous snakes only. I have known rewards in large numbers paid in a district for the harmless Lycodon, and I am by no means sure that the disbursing official was, in the end, convinced that the object of his persecution was harmless. Still, in another district where a perfectly competent officer supervised the distribution, the snakes were brought in in undiminished numbers while the reward was given. It is, of course, likely that they were brought in from greater distances, as no reward was given in the surrounding districts. On this subject, therefore, there is not sufficient evidence. But universal experience shows us that when man has earnestly striven to extirpate a noxious animal he has always succeeded. Deaths from snake-bite used to be common in Europe, they are almost unknown at present; and the same thing may be said of North America. Wolves are now exceedingly rare in Southern and Eastern Europe, where they used to constitute a public danger. It is only amidst a passive population that pests of this kind are tolerated.

That snakes are most frequently found in jungles and similar places is of course accurate, but that natives are bitten there is certainly not true. The most striking feature in the statistics of death from snake-bite is the exceeding frequency with which women are bitten. Thus, in Bengal, in the last year for which I have the detailed statistics, 2,155 women were killed, for 2,040 men, and no less than sixteen per cent. of the deaths were of children under ten years of age. In other words, the home-staying portion of the population suffered as heavily as those going abroad. But nearly twice as many persons were bitten during the night as during the day, showing still more clearly that the calamity takes place, not in the jungle, but actually in the home. The mortality from snake-bite in India does not depend upon the snakes in the jungle, but the presence of these reptiles amongst the very people, who take not even the ordinary precautions against being bitten. It is the indifference of the people to the presence of these enemies in their very midst that produces the fearful loss of life in India. The toleration accorded to snakes is simply incredible. A native, to my knowledge, has allowed a poisonous reptile to escape that had fatally bitten a member of his family. The attitude of the Indian peasant towards poisonous snakes may be described as that of passive toleration to avoid their active enmity. Sometimes, indeed, it even goes further than this, and snakes are offered food to propitiate them. On this ground alone it would seem wise to follow up a policy that would tend to rouse in the native mind an idea of resistance and hostility.

But may not the reward stimulate the inhabitants to breed snakes, and not to catch them? Means as far as possible have been taken to obtain information on this subject. I have bred cobras, and have found it a work of great difficulty. If the eggs become too dry, development is suspended; if they are made too moist, it is stopped altogether. They require, therefore, great attention. When the young cobra is hatched it is very small, very irritable, and exceedingly dangerous. A full-grown cobra can be handled with perfect safety, but a young one, ten or eleven inches long, is so active, and its body is so small, that it can be scarcely touched with impunity. I have seen hundreds of cobras brought in for rewards, but yearlings have been very few amongst them. The reason is that when the snake's hole is dug out, the cobra with the long body can be readily seized; but the young one, which can turn round in the smallest space with the greatest ease, is generally allowed to escape. The fact that yearlings are seldom brought in for the reward is conclusive evidence that it does not answer to breed them, for no one would seriously urge that the breeder would keep them for a long time before producing them.

Taken altogether, then, it would seem wise to adopt a moderate system of rewards; but attention, of course, should be paid to every detail that can add efficiency to the scheme, and lessen its cost. In no case should a reward be given except for a poisonous snake, and the officer in charge of the distribution should, in all cases, be thoroughly competent to identify *all* common snakes, both poisonous and non-poisonous; a knowledge that can be acquired with ease in a few days, or even hours, if opportunities of inspecting the snakes themselves be afforded. It is doubtful, also, whether rewards should be given for all poisonous snakes. The *Trimeresuri*, for instance, are not very dangerous to life, and perhaps no advantage would be gained by including them. The snakes in the front rank of those offending, probably in the order of their danger, are the Cobra, the Bungarus cœruleus, the Echis carinata, the Daboia russellii, the

Bungarus fasciatus, and the Ophiophagus elaps, and rewards should only be given for these. The above arrangement is, of course, one of probability only, as statistics throw little or no light on the matter.

Great attention should be paid to the conservancy of small towns and villages. In large towns public opinion is already awake to the injury inflicted by jungle being allowed to grow up around dwellings; but in villages, naturally, but little attention is given to a detail of this kind. A few holes stopped, and a few bushes cut down in every village, would diminish immensely the hiding-places of these pests, and exactly at the spots where they do most harm.

That municipalities have in many cases undertaken to give rewards for the destruction of snakes is a sign of great hopefulness.

The most stringent system that has yet been devised to exterminate pests is undoubtedly that of requiring the inhabitants of an infested district either to present a certain number of the proscribed animals each year or to pay a sum instead, the amount thus obtained being devoted to the purposes of extermination. It is difficult to see how any animal, however prolific, could withstand a persecution of this kind. But, of course, a scheme like this presupposes that the inhabitants should clearly see that it is their real advantage that is being consulted, and that they have no reluctance to destroy their foes.

Another consideration to be regarded is, whether there is any special season in which snakes can be destroyed with advantage. In the cold weather the reptiles are torpid, and do little or no injury; but from March to September the loss of human life steadily increases. The rainy season, commencing at the end of June, driving them from their holes, naturally increases the mortality greatly. It might, therefore, be assumed that the rainy season is the period when they should be chiefly attacked. But if we study the natural history of the cobra, we shall find that the female usually lays her eggs in July. The great aim, therefore, should be to destroy as many of the reptiles as possible before the eggs are laid, remembering that every female captured then is equal to very many later on, and that vipers, which, of course, bring forth their young alive, are even much more prolific. The months, therefore, of May and June, and part of July, are those in which the destruction of snakes is likely to be attended with the greatest results. This would, in fact, be inverting the policy of a "close season," which has been found so successful all over the world in favouring the production of game.

The amount to be paid for each snake must clearly depend upon the cost of labour locally. Practically, but little difficulty can be experienced in determining it, as an insufficient sum will have no result in causing snakes to be brought in. But the effect of any system could, in regard to its ultimate success, not be ascertained at once. In this, as in most other things, a policy to have any effect must be persevered in. Seasons fluctuate greatly, and though, of course, averages must show in the end whether progress is being made, yet increased accuracy in registration together with the varying nature of the climate, may prevent the result being speedily manifest.

It is sometimes stated that the loss of life from snake-bite in India is exaggerated by the neighbours being induced to return cases of murder as dying from this cause. But it should be remembered that in all cases of supposed snake-bite, the body is brought for examination to an English official, and the circumstances undergo close scrutiny; whereas, if the death were reported as being of a more usual nature no investigation would follow. It is hardly likely that murderers would assign a cause which would at once challenge inquiry. I have examined many bodies of persons supposed to have died from snake-bite, and in all cases, either from the blood, or from the wounded place itself, by macerating it in water, I have obtained sufficient poison to produce all the symptoms. Besides, as stated before, the appearances are quite characteristic. There is no reason to suppose, therefore, that the loss of life is in the least degree smaller than is represented. But in regard to loss of property from destruction of cattle and domestic animals, immense though it is reported to be, it is probably but a small part of that which really occurs, for the peasant has no motive to report his loss; he obtains no compensation, and a visit to a thánà would be naturally looked upon as a disagreeable task; and so the loss is borne in the silence so characteristic of the race when in adversity.

INDEX.

A

B

C

D

E

F

G

H

I

K

L

M

N

O

P

R

S

T